PERFECT
PHRASES
for
PROFESSIONAL
NETWORKING

PERFECT PHRASES

for

PROFESSIONAL NETWORKING

**Hundreds of Ready-to-Use Phrases for Meeting
and Keeping Helpful Contacts—
Everywhere You Go**

Susan Benjamin

New York   Chicago   San Francisco   Lisbon   London   Madrid   Mexico City
Milan   New Delhi   San Juan   Seoul   Singapore   Sydney   Toronto

The *McGraw·Hill* Companies

Library of Congress Cataloging-in-Publication Data

Benjamin, Susan, 1957–
    Perfect phrases for professional networking : hundreds of ready-to-use
    phrases for meeting and keeping helpful contacts--everywhere you go / by
    Susan F. Benjamin.
        p.   cm.
    ISBN-13: 978-0-07-162916-4 (alk. paper)
    1. Business networks.   2. Business communication.   I. Title.

HD69.S8B457   2009
651.7—dc22   2009027025

1 2 3 4 5 6 7 8 9 10 11 12 13 14 15 16 17 18 19 20 21 23   FGR/FGR 0 9

ISBN 978-0-07-162916-4
MHID   0-07-162916-5

McGraw-Hill books are available at special quantity discounts to use as premiums and
sales promotions or for use in corporate training programs. To contact a representative,
please e-mail us at bulksales@mcgraw-hill.com.

Contents

Contents

Contents

Contents

Acknowledgments

I love the acknowledgment section of my book—it's so much fun to sit down and name names. What's most interesting is that many of the names change, but a lot of them stay the same, too.

So, to risk redundancy, I'll start by acknowledging those many people who (fortunately) don't or won't go away. First, my husband, Dan, and my son, Adam. What can I say? What can I ever say? They give me the space and the humor that is vital to my writing. I couldn't network about networking, or much else, without it.

Then there's my agent, Grace Freedson. She's practically a sister at this point, always pulling for my career and the sprouting of new and challenging books. And she struck gold when she said, "How about a book on networking?" And naturally, thanks to the folks at McGraw-Hill. This is my third Perfect Phrases book; they're really fun to write, and I look forward to hearing more from readers all over the globe.

And who could forget my proofreader, Libby Howard, who doesn't complain about my millions of typing mistakes. Thanks, Libby, for that and the details you fixed under my usual can-I-have-this-tomorrow type of deadline. Then there's Erika Ostergard, my assistant and accomplice in all sorts of buzz-related, if not inspiring, crimes. Off with the Peace Corps on new and even more dynamic (if that's possible!) experiences. And speaking of which—thanks to my assistant and my cohort in radio crimes Ashley and to David Wolf, who's been networking with me for ages!

Perhaps the best "working" of all has nothing to do with working, so thanks to all those folks who have plugged me into everything from homeschooling opportunities to publishers. Lissa Brown—yes, you!—and Lucy Jenkins, of the French persuasion. They gave me the opportunity to explore networking from new directions. It's been great!

As the old saying goes, couldn't have done it without you!

Oh, and here's one more perfect phrase from Kitty Clarke, my dance teacher: Whatever you do, do it with conviction. That's what makes all those phrases truly perfect!

Part 1

Perfect Phrases for Networking in Any Situation

So many situations, so much networking. What's a well-intended networker to do? Especially when the timing, expectations, and personalities of those involved vary extensively? Well, there's good news and bad news.

Let's get the bad news out of the way first. In the real-life world of networking, there aren't a whole lot of rules outside of the obvious, such as no swearing, no stealing, and keep your clothes on. Aside from that, how you respond is individual: you must be adept at getting a feel for the situation and determine what will work to your—and everyone else's—advantage.

Now for the good news: There aren't rules, but there are plenty of guidelines that will help. For example, you should always be sincere. As tempting as it might be, avoid being insincere or unduly complimentary. You'll come off as phony. When you're talking to a prime networking target, be alert for body language. Someone who glances at the clock is saying it's time to put a stopper on the conversation.

This section will provide even more guidelines to help you steer through the exciting, interesting, and often muddy waters of networking.

Chapter 1

The Basics

Networking can be a rather nerve-racking experience. And with good reason, too. Normally when you meet people, you're more or less equals. You go to a cocktail party and that guy or gal is nursing a drink, right? And so are you. Maybe you chat. Get into a discussion. And why not, you're guests. What else should you be doing?

But when you're networking, you're not equal; you want something from the other person. You need to charm him or her, make a great impression, and get what you're after. And unless you're going to one of those meetings that is explicitly dedicated to networking, that person may not have a whole lot to get from you. So, you have to seem natural and nonchalant even though, well, you're not!

So, what *are* you supposed to do? Here's a list—we'll add the perfect phrases later.

Networking: The List

- **Relax.** I know, I know—telling people to relax is the fastest way to make them tense. Just like when the dentist tells you to uncross your legs and relax as he or she points a needle the size of a fishhook into your mouth. But I mean it. The tenser you are, the more stilted your language will become and the less convincing you'll sound.

- **Personalize.** The networking opportunity is about people—you and whomever you're networking with. So, it's critical that you create a personal relationship. And this means you need to know something about that person. What is her history? Her interests? Why should she care enough about you to pass on information—be it names, organizations, or just insights and ideas? I'm not suggesting you have to research everyone you network with—after all, if you're at a party with a networking group, this is probably impossible. But when it comes time to send that follow-up e-mail or notice, go right ahead and Google.

- **Have courage.** Even the most experienced salesperson will tell you that networking requires a deep breath or two, especially when the people you're contacting are well positioned. By that I mean, they have the power to make your life much easier, richer, or otherwise better. But don't sweat it. Just keep your mind in the present as much as possible: make that contact and don't worry about what will happen if you blow it. (P.S. Everyone *does* blow it now and then. And guess what? Where that one all-important networking opportunity died, about ten more crop up.)

- **See value.** In most networking situations, contacts may seem like helpers—people who pass on gobs of information as you take, take, take. What's in it for them? Or, more to the point, how dare you be so selfish, demanding, and . . . OK, wait. You're not. Really. So blast that thought out of your head. In fact, you're bringing value to these people on two fronts.
  - You're giving them the satisfaction of helping you and possibly the person they're introducing you to. I know this sounds only so-so valuable, but actually playing a positive force can be quite the motivating factor in any relationship.

Obviously, you need to thank them afterward—and later, too—but that's for another chapter.

- Whatever you bring them in return. One of the core elements of our social agreements, albeit unspoken, is the concept of reciprocity or, in more common terms, you scratch my back and I'll scratch yours. So, you need to offer them something in return. And not, "If I can help you out, just let me know . . ." Something concrete and of real value to them.

- **Remember the stakes.** When networking, the stakes are high for you—and your contacts. For example, if your contacts pass on the name of another contact, they're putting their reputation on the line, too. If you make a positive impression, you're sending a positive message about them. If you're a jerk (not that you would ever be, of course!), that reflects negatively on them as well. So it's critical that in all your networking interactions, you project the most positive, professional, and trust-inspiring impression possible. Dress nicely, on all occasions—or, more to the point, dress appropriately for all occasions. Going to a football game with boundless networking opportunities? Don't wear a suit and tie, of course; that would be weird. But do wear good jeans and a clean, well-fitted parka. If you're sending an e-mail, make sure your grammar is impeccable and don't take too many liberties—at least, not yet. Smiley faces, such as :), are out. Letters only, as in R U OK?—also out. Full sentences, definitely in.

- **Put away the "want."** OK, when most people network, it's because they want something. A job. Money. A girlfriend, boyfriend, or business connection. Sometimes you're needy, and sometimes you're *really* needy, and sometimes, well, *panicky* comes to mind. Regardless of how you're feeling, put that emotion away. People can smell desperation: it's strong, present, and unappealing. And networking begins with an interaction as simple as a handshake. So, what do you do? Put the fear away and spring into action. Meet, greet, and hope for the best. And whatever happens, happens.

One more *very* important point: the most crucial part of networking, beyond all else, is your immediate impression. That's true whether you're e-mailing, calling on the phone, shaking hands, or even just meeting someone's eyes from across the room. That first impression occurs in a flash. If you're writing or calling, it could make or break the entire interaction. If you're meeting in person, with the benefits of body language and other signals, you may, just may, be able to turn a negative impression around.

So, read on and use these upcoming perfect phrases to make your first hello a lasting—or at least a recurring—one!

A Quick Look at Networking Dos and Don'ts

People have been networking since the beginning of time. Moses leading his people through the Red Sea? Networking. Sholomo knew Aaron, brother of Moses. They talked a little, networked, and Sholomo shook Moses' hand. Before you knew it, they were on their way to the Holy Land.

But through the ages of networking, some pretty bad habits have surfaced. Take those networking phrases that fall into phone calls, e-mails, conversation as easily as olives from a tree. They're so available. So natural. So time-tested. Except that they sound insincere, disingenuous, and generally boring. Here are some of those tiresome phrases:

Per Mary Dawson's recommendation, I am contacting you . . .

Please note the enclosed letters of recommendation . . .

Thanks for your time yesterday.

I am sending you this e-mail on the recommendation of . . .

I will tailor my efforts . . .

I can meet the needs . . .

Instead, try to use the most casual and specific language possible (while still being very polite, of course). The more specific you are about what you have to offer, the more likely your contact will network on your behalf and provide the leads and ideas that will be helpful to you:

Our mutual friend Mary Dawson suggested that I contact you.

I am sending along a few letters of recommendation.

Thanks for the information you gave me yesterday. I plan to contact everyone on the list immediately.

I regularly handled at least thirty clients a day and was able to address their concerns in an agreed-upon time frame.

Don't focus on yourself: no one cares about your personal life. OK, your mother and maybe your kids and your partner or spouse might care, but when it comes to networking, people care about themselves or some issue, idea, or opportunity that intrigues them—so you want to show them how you fit into that. Avoid self-focusing first phrases like these:

I want to talk to you because . . .

Mary said I should connect with you because I want . . .

I'm looking for a job and wanted to get . . .

I've been really upset lately because of the economy and thought you could give me . . . [This approach should be used only with your therapist!]

Instead, focus on them: compliment, intrigue, make them feel generally good. Notice the difference:

I know that you are an expert in our field, and I was hoping you would discuss . . .

Mary said you're among the most respected people in the field and might be willing to give me advice . . .

Since you're an expert in this industry, I was hoping you could point me in the right direction . . .

You're probably the best source for ways to navigate the difficult economy, and I thought you could advise me . . .

Granted, you do run the risk of seeming insincere. The best way around that, though, is to truly mean what you say. If the guy really is a renowned expert, say it. If not, figure out what he really is. Well respected? Well informed? Knowledgeable? Then use those types of adjectives.

Don't expect your contact will remember you:

Hi, this is me [or whatever your name is]. Just calling to let you know my progress since we talked.

I just wanted to follow up and tell you that I got the job at the university.

I wanted to shoot you a quick note to let you know I joined the networking association.

I spoke to Rose and she sends her regards. She gave me lots of useful information, and I appreciate your help in connecting me.

Who are you? When did you meet or speak? If you only met once, spoke on the phone, traded e-mails, or whatever, chances are this person forgot you. Don't take it personally. She's busy. She doesn't remember her own kids, on a bad day. So, you need to remind her. But be discreet. She may be forgetful, but that doesn't mean she *realizes* she's forgetful!

Do remind your contact of who you are:

Thanks for referring me to Janet Johnson at the networking meeting in Chicago last month. I spoke with her a few days ago and she sends her regards.

Just wanted you to know that I joined the networking organization, as you suggested in our phone conversation last month. As I mentioned, I was laid off by the MARC Corporation but am now optimistic about finding a job.

When we spoke three weeks ago, I was looking for a job. Thanks to your recommendation that I contact Alfred, I found one!

I hope you've been well since we met at the convention last fall. At that time, I was looking for customers for my new Perfect Tool. Thanks to your suggestions, I now have . . .

Don't demand—even politely. It's bad enough when someone you love makes demands. But it's a total turnoff when someone you don't know makes demands *and* wants a favor, such as a networking connection.

Don't be abrupt:

I think you can give me the names I need . . .

I want lists of . . .

I need some names from you.

Give me some information.

I would like you to get me a contact list for . . .

Because you are so well positioned, I want you to . . .

I think you should . . .

Please get me the names as soon as possible.

I am in a hurry, so you need to respond quickly.

I want thirty minutes of your time.

Do be appreciative and flexible:

Would you be willing to send me those names?

Is it OK if you send more of those names?

If you could get me the contact list, I would be most appreciative.

Because you are so well positioned, I thought you could provide some helpful information. Would that be possible?

Whenever you can get me those names would be great. I'm working as hard as I can and am ready.

Could I have thirty minutes of your time?

People love to help other people, so be sure to use these and similar words:

Give advice

Point me to

Provide me with

Advise me

Help me

Don't forget to thank them, and do it outright:

I appreciate your insights.

Thanks for the ideas you presented in our discussion.

Thank you for passing along that list of contacts.

I appreciate your meeting with me on Friday.

Then let your contact know what aspect of the discussion was especially helpful. Be as specific as you can:

I never knew about those associations, although I've been in the industry for about twenty years.

I've read a great deal on the subject, but you're the first to offer those insights.

Those names will prove invaluable.

I really needed a shot in the arm: your enthusiasm was great!

Whenever possible, show your contact how you followed up:

I've reviewed the associations' websites, as you recommended, and found two of them that would be immensely helpful to me!

I'm building your ideas into my sales plan.

My assistant and I will begin contacting them immediately.

I'm planning to start calling first thing in the morning.

Address the Person, Not the Opportunity

When communicating, especially in writing, you may have the urge to sound formal, overly professional, or really, really smart. Don't bother.

In the networking universe, your greatest advantage is to strike up a strong relationship with the person you're addressing. This means, of course, that you shouldn't *try* to be anything, except yourself.

But, as we all know, communications aren't as simple as that. Because who you are is a multifaceted thing. Think about who you are in front of your boss. Then, in front of your lover. Now, in front of your parents. Different, right? So, you need to address whomever you're networking with as naturally and personally as possible, depending on your relationship with them.

Be natural by using words that are appropriately formal or informal:

To a peer:
How are you doing?

It would be really cool if we could share some ideas about the company.

Do you know any good contacts? Maybe we can exchange some names.

Have any insights into the executive team? I was hoping to get invited to one of their forums.

To an expert in the field:
How are you?

I would appreciate any insights into the company.

I'd be happy to pass along anything that might be helpful to you, as well.

Of course, you don't want to use language that isn't really "you," so stick with your own style, tailored to your audience.

Discuss or draw personal connections:

I noticed that you lived in Boston—so did I, in 1992.

In the picture on your website, you're sitting beside a German shepherd. I have one, too. They're great dogs, aren't they?

Did you ever read Tom Peters? What do you think of his business ideas?

You went to Princeton? So did I. But only for a summer!

Avoid the passive voice. If you don't remember what the passive voice is, look it up in a good grammar book or look at your e-mails to friends. With the passive voice, you omit the noun or pronoun that refers to the person who is doing the action, as if the event or discussion occurred on its own. This is common in business or otherwise formal communications. Unfortunately, you may unconsciously resort to the passive voice in networking communications as well. Do not use the impersonal and corporate-sounding passive voice:

A list of excellent restaurants is enclosed, as a thank-you for all your great insights last week.

After our discussion, Jane and Henry were called, per your recommendation.

Pursuant to our last conversation: the main office was moved last week. Thought you'd like to know.

The application was received last week!

In relaxed, friendly conversation, you would naturally use the active voice, which clearly indicates who did what:

I'm sending you a list of excellent restaurants as a thank-you for all your great insights last week.

After our discussion, I called Jane and Henry as you recommended.

Just wanted to follow up on our last conversation: the president decided to move the main office. Thought you'd like to know.

I received the application last week!

Use questions and other engaging language when it seems natural and doesn't demand much from your audience:

I'm originally from Oregon. Have you ever been there?

Did you happen to read the Kentucky report?

Today's speaker worked at Smith and Sons for eight years. Do you know them?

Our product is a combination of mustard and gel sauce. Have you tried it?

The scene at the convention reminded me of the movie Shark. *Did you see it?*

Then, get back to the original point, unless the other person wants to pursue the personal talk further. Remember: it's these personal interactions that make contacts more likely to open up to you and follow up should new ideas occur to them.

Pointer: When forging a relationship, try not to focus too much on yourself. In their eyes, you may not be that interesting. But should you focus on them instead? That depends. Some people, maybe most people, love to talk about themselves, especially when they feel that they're being admired. But many don't. They may feel shy or that their privacy has been intruded on. The best way to tell is to look at their body language—do they appear open or closed?—and gauge how readily they respond.

Give Them a Chance to Respond Honestly

You know what you want your contacts to give you: names, ideas, and leads. But remember, just by asking you can make them feel either valued or pressured. You can make them feel open and willing to say yes or embarrassed by having to say no. Your job is to allow contacts to respond honestly, or not at all.

These perfect phrases give your contacts wiggle room they'll appreciate:

Do: *Would you happen to know anyone at the company I can contact?*

Don't: *Who should I contact at the company?*

Do: *Can you recommend anyone who might enjoy our product?*

Don't: *Who should I contact about our product?*

Do: *I'd like to meet the folks in your group. Would that be possible?*

Don't: *I'd like to meet the folks in your group. When should I come in?*

If your contacts seem reserved, hesitant, or embarrassed, let them off easy with one of these perfect phrases:

Don't worry if you have to say no.

I don't want to intrude; do you think that will be a problem?

If you'd like to get back to me, that's fine.

Any insights would be helpful.

Are you OK with my asking?

You can also reassure them that they won't regret the connection:

I'll be sure to call only during business hours.

If you think it's best, I'll drop an e-mail, then let them get in touch if they want to.

I never send unwanted messages. If they want off the list, I'll take them off immediately.

Use your contact's name when you get in touch with the person he or she recommended, but only with permission. This will reassure the lead and save you and your contact possible embarrassment. In some cases, for example, your contact can recommend great leads, but those leads may not know or even like your contact!

Ask your contact for permission to use his or her name:

May I mention that you said to get in touch?

OK if I use your name?

Can I use you as a reference?

I'd like to tell them you said to call—do you mind?

Follow Up, Follow Up, Follow Up

Update your contacts about your progress. Stay in touch, especially as you move forward. Be sure to draw connections between their efforts and your progress whenever possible.

I have an interview for the job at IT International. Thanks for suggesting it.

I met with Laura last week. She gave me lots of great leads. I really appreciate your introduction.

Things seem to have turned around since we spoke. In fact, it looks like our profits are actually up.

We put your idea to good use. After we contacted Scott, we found we had several new customers!

One last point on the basics. These days you have countless networking venues: online social networks, virtual networks, old-fashioned face-to-face meetings, e-mails—you know the list. Be sure to do your networking in a venue that most suits (and attracts) the contacts you most want to meet.

Similarly, if you're contacting someone directly, whether in a follow-up or a first hello, be sure to use the right method. If you're networking with a Gen Y, roughly age thirty or under, for example, then e-mails and text messaging work well. But if you're connecting with a midlife baby boomer, although e-mail is probably OK, it may be better to just call on the telephone.

Chapter 2

The First Hello

So, why spend an entire chapter on the first hello? Because that initial moment is of critical importance to your networking opportunity. Here's why: people tend to form immediate, subconscious responses to others. Particularly if you're writing, whether an e-mail or a formal letter, that first response may be indelible. In fact, some researchers say that visitors determine what they think of a website in less time than it takes to blink their eyes. After that, the halo effect kicks in, meaning that initial feeling never completely wears off.

If you're meeting someone at a conference or at a friend's house, the situation is somewhat different. Off to a rocky start? You may be able to read their body language, adjust accordingly, and help make good of a bad impression. Still, whether face-to-face, on the phone, or in writing, make sure that first hello really counts.

Leverage Relationships

One of your primary tasks when forging that first connection is to get the contacts' attention. This may seem easy, but it isn't. Each day your contacts, like most of us, are bombarded with 4,000 to 7,000 messages through various channels. Metaphorically, your message is a grain of sand on a sandy shore. So, think Day-Glo pink: jazzy, snappy, and bold, bold, bold. In other words, your message must stand out from all the others.

Of course, you don't want to be obnoxious or inappropriately energetic, either. Instead, win them over with charm, authenticity (yes, you can be authentically charming!), and a personal touch. Use a personal connection whenever possible—starting with your referral's name first.

Do not:

I am writing because Betty Smith said you might be able to help me in my job search.

This e-mail is in regards to my current job search. My friend Pete Simms thought you might be able to help.

I'm contacting you because Harriet Meyers thought you might have some good contacts for my organization "Friends of Dogs."

Do:

Betty Smith suggested that I contact you . . .

Pete Simms recommended that I e-mail you . . .

Harriet Meyers thought I should contact you . . .

If you're not sure how well your contacts know or will remember your referral, remind them. Be subtle:

Our mutual friend Betty Smith suggested that I contact you.

Harriet Meyers, of the Humane Society in Los Angeles, suggested that I contact you about my organization, "Friends of Dogs."

Pete Simms, whom you met in Bermuda last spring, recommended that I e-mail you.

Add more detail or go to great lengths describing the relationship (or even a few extra words), and you risk insulting the contact. (Harriet? Of course I know Harriet. I'm not *that* out of it!)

If you think your contacts know the person referring you but may have trouble immediately remembering who that person is, slip in information about the relationship using a word or two:

> *Your cousin, Nancy, recommended that I call you.*

> *Your co-worker, Margaret, passed along your contact information.*

> *Your mother's friend, Laura, said I should get in touch with you.*

Notice that you're only using the person's first name here. The closeness of the relationship doesn't require that you use more.

Next, in the most specific terms possible, let your contacts know why you're approaching them:

> *She thought you might have a list of potential donors in this area whom we could contact.*

> *He said you may be able to give me insights into Corporate Giant. We're hoping to bid on an important project and would like as many insights as possible.*

> *My mother told her I was hoping to make some social connections, as I'm new in town.*

If you don't have a personal connection, explain how you found the contact's name. Keep it as familiar and personal as possible. Do **not** let it sound like a mass-mailer, even if you are mass-mailing.

Do not:

I'm writing because I am looking for a new job.

I was interested in learning more about your donor list.

I am a . . .

As a _____ [your title or interest here], I was hoping you could help me.

I'm contacting you because . . . [Face it, who cares?]

I'm looking for the CEO/president/hiring person . . . [So, what is that person on the other end of the line? To paraphrase Barbra Streisand, "Chopped liver?"]

Do:

As a fellow member of the Clean-up Club, I found your name in this year's directory.

I found your contact information online: I was really impressed with your website and had to call.

I read your article in Today's Times *and was hoping we could talk about . . .*

As an ardent reader of science fiction, I have been reading your works for at least ten years. In fact, you've influenced me so much I actually wrote a book recently and have published numerous short stories. I was wondering if you could recommend a good agent.

Get Personal

You don't want to give away too much when discussing yourself with contacts. What if they're not interested? What if they're not the chatty type? Still, the more personal and interactive the comment, the better. So, you need to find a balance. Here are a few situations and perfect phrases that illustrate this idea best.

Situation: You see a woman at a networking meeting with a dress that you happen to own.

Oh, I have that same dress. Did you get it at Saks?

That dress is so comfortable! I know, I have it!

Situation: A potential contact is wearing a cap with your hometown, let's say, Boston, on it.

Are you a Sox fan?

Are you from Boston? I grew up there.

Situation: They're reading a book you just finished.

How do you like that book? I just finished it.

Oh, look—John Grisham. He's a good writer. I just finished that book.

Easy, right? Let the conversation take its natural course and gradually introduce the networking angle:

So, why are you attending this convention?

Do you work for Levy Corps?

I see from your name tag that you're an official. How long have you been part of the association?

Factors in the environment can also lead to a nice opening comment in a face-to-face meeting.

Is it my imagination, or is it really cold in here?

Did you see that lightning last night?

Do you see how many people attended this conference? I heard about six thousand.

Hope you've survived the snowstorm.

What did you think of the keynote speaker last night?

If you're an expert in your field, you want contacts to recognize your stature, but you don't want to brag. So, try to relate your feats to something else. Here are a few subtle ways to do that:

I notice that you're reading **The Life Cycle of the Fruit Fly.**
I wrote an article about the fruit fly that was published in
Biology Today.

It's great that Stan Minx won the Prestige Award. I received it
in 2005 and it really shaped the opportunities that lay before
me.

Are you an attorney? So am I. In fact, I won the Bar Award last
month.

Or in writing:

As the winner of the Bar Award, I can provide invaluable
insights to the members of your networking group.

I was selected Presenter of the Year because I offer great
advice to professionals like your members in an upbeat and
humorous way.

If you're sending a follow-up e-mail to remind them to send leads or ask for more information, you can always start with an opener that reminds them of where you met—and strikes a personal note.

I hope you've been well since the RTIR conference in
New York.

Great meeting you at the Wine Grows Expo in Dallas.

Thanks for your insights at the Club Conference in Santa Fe.

Then follow with a more specific note:

> *Hope you made it to your plane without any problem. The traffic was fierce. [This one's perfect if you met on the shuttle to the airport.]*

> *Did you have a chance to sample the new vintage when you got home?*

> *I looked up those concepts you suggested—there's a lot to explore!*

> *After our conversation about asphalt supply in the U.S., I researched some more about it. In fact, builders are predicting a shortage.*

> *I looked into the facts we received at the meeting; they were inaccurate, but only by 3 per cent.*

> *I'm attaching the article I told you about at lunch—hope you find it helpful.*

Regardless of exactly what you say, keep the openers short—a line or two is enough. Then, get to the point.

Use Humor to Break the Ice

Humor can be easy—or extremely tricky! So, before you use humor to start a conversation at a conference, networking event, or party, make sure of the following:

- The contact is ripe and ready for a humorous remark. You can tell this by doing a smile check. You smile and if the contact smiles back, go ahead.
- The humor flows naturally from the situation. Nothing's more awkward than a joke that flies out at you from nowhere.

- The humor must be appropriate. Jokes about other people—out. Dirty jokes—out. Mean or controversial jokes—out. Subtle, ironic, or otherwise suitable jokes—in.

Here are a few examples of when to use humor:

Situation: **When you trip over a cord or even just trip.**

Oh, that was graceful.

My mother always said I should be a ballerina.

Thank you. [Then bow.]

I meant to do that.

Situation: **When the person next to you is reading a book and looks up to nod or smile at you.**

Ever hear that Groucho Marx line, "Outside of a dog, a book is a man's best friend. Inside a dog, it's too dark to read"? Funny, isn't it?

You know what book just came out? The collected works of George Carlin. Can you imagine what's in that? [This should lead to some humorous memories of Carlin and create a nice bond between you.]

You can also use humor to open a brochure or portion of your website when you're trying to generate leads from it. One of the best ways to do this is to quote a humorist, either as a call-out or in the middle of the text. Since it stands out, the contact will likely see it first. Here are some humorous quotes—you can get endless others online:

"I don't know who my grandfather was; I am much more concerned to know who his grandson will be."
—Abraham Lincoln [for an educator]

"Hell hath no fury like a hustler with a literary agency."
—Frank Sinatra [for a bookseller, author, agent]

"All I need is room enough to lay a hat and a few friends."
—Dorothy Parker [for fun-loving women's groups. Hint: Only use when assured the contacts will appreciate the content!]

You can also embed your quote into the text:

As Albert Einstein once said, "If you are out to describe the truth, leave elegance to the tailor." We agree . . .

As Garfield the cat once said: "I'm hungry; therefore I am." As a caterer, I've fed thousands of hungry and appreciative eaters and am craving to work for . . .

If it's true that "man invented language to satisfy his deep need to complain," as Lily Tomlin once said, then customer service specialists must be the ultimate listeners.

If your interaction has a natural humorous note, run with it. Nothing solidifies a relationship more. If you're a more introverted or serious type, don't feel obliged to enter humor into your interaction. Stay with whatever is natural to you.

Cut Through Coldness to Break the Ice

What do you do when your contact is all but ignoring you? Your natural reaction when addressing a cold or indifferent contact is to duck away or, as they say, run for shelter. Who wants to hang around the coldness, which generally signals disapproval? Who wants to enter the freezing waters of a conversation that stops? Actually, you do, if that person can provide you with the names, ideas, and places that will help in your search. So, what's a networker to do to break the ice? Here are a few ideas:

Enter cautiously with a comment or two:

Do you mind if I interrupt for a moment?

Excuse me . . .

I don't want to break your train of thought, but could you tell me . . .

If you don't mind, I was wondering . . .

At this point, body language is key. If the person glances up with a long sigh, or crosses her arms over her midsection, keep it short and leave it up to her to carry the conversation further. If the person turns to you full-face, with arms at his sides or held loosely by the body, pursue the discussion.

Find a connection:

I noticed you were reading Seedlings Today. *I just renewed my subscription; it's really informational, don't you think?*

I saw you were just talking to Sandy Spear. She was an employee of mine about ten years ago when she was just entering aerodynamics.

Compliments are always a plus:

I attended your presentation earlier—it was really great.

I really liked what you said to Joe at the last meeting. Did he bring it up later?

I know you're an expert in the formative development of primates. So, I was interested in your insights about . . .

Ask questions:

What did you think of the speaker?

Do you know which sessions you'll attend later?

Who is the host of this networking party? We haven't met.

Have you been to one of these before?

Is that your magazine? I heard there was an interesting article about the drying time of cement in cold weather.

From there, move the conversation over to the networking information you need. When in doubt about whether the ice is entirely broken or just temporarily chipped, give your contact an opening and see what happens.

Find an opening:

I was hoping to get the names of some contacts at the plant.

I was interested in attending their gatherings but wasn't sure about the best way to get an invitation.

If the meetings are by invitation only, how would a newcomer get in?

I'm interested in speaking to some of them.

And remember, when all else fails, move on!

Attire helpers. Attire, in a networking situation, speaks louder than words. So, be sure that you represent yourself as well as possible. Although you want to dress for the occasion (don't wear a tux at a beer bash), it's better to overdress than underdress.

Chapter 3

Asking for Leads

So the conversation started off OK, but how do you leave the universe of chitchat and actually ask for leads? We touched on this a bit in the last section—let's take a closer look.

One of the most difficult aspects of networking for many otherwise confident and sociable professionals, or even effervescent newcomers, is asking for something. You open the conversation. No problem. You hit it off. Great. But how do you put yourself at their mercy? Be vulnerable? Ask for something they have and you need? For many of us, our upbringing and culture just don't give us those tools.

Before you jump into the networking scene, remind yourself of two key points. First, most people enjoy helping others; it makes them feel good about themselves and positions them as experts. Second, every good deed demands a return. In other words, offer them something back, and if they accept, give generously.

Remember, your contact may put you off for reasons you may never know. Perhaps she is on bad terms with the person you have in common. Perhaps he's too busy to give you the attention you need to make those connections meaningful. Or, perhaps she simply isn't well positioned enough, or knowledgeable enough, to pass on the information you seek.

Regardless, stay tuned for the perfect phrases that will help you delicately step through the mire of favor asking to find gleaming rewards!

Steering the Conversation to Leads

So, there you are, having a really pleasant personal conversation with someone about kids, homes, pets, and so forth. Now how do you shift the conversation to discuss the all-important subject matter: you?

Use a few transition words:

By the way . . .

A minute ago you mentioned that . . .

Since you mentioned _____ I was wondering . . .

I wanted to ask you . . .

Oh, do you mind if I ask . . .

I was wondering . . .

Here are some examples of how these phrases appear in conversation:

You mentioned that you worked for the Stevens Company. Do you happen to know who's in charge of purchasing there?

Now that you mention Dover, I was thinking of applying for a position in their accounting department. Do you know anyone there?

Since you've been in the company for twenty years, I wonder if you know the best way for me to reach the head of accounting.

Since you work for Dow and Dow, I wondered if you knew how I could get hold of a company directory.

Sometimes the conversation doesn't lead to a simple transition. So you may need to be more direct—without being abrupt.

Do you mind if I move on to another subject for a minute?

I hope you don't mind my asking . . .

I did want to ask you . . .

By the way, I may have mentioned that I was job hunting. Would you know . . .

Not to change the subject but . . .

Would you happen to know . . .

You may get asked this a lot, but . . .

Asking for Leads Directly

Go ahead, just ask. But make sure your contacts are open, friendly, and obviously willing to help. And be careful to *ask*—not demand. Demands make absolutely imperfect phrases!

Do not:
I want the names of people I can contact, and I know you have some good ones.

Tell me who to contact.

Why don't you call them and see if I can attend.

I'd like you to send me those lists by Friday.

Do:
Do you know anyone I can contact in that organization?

Where do you recommend I go for more information?

Do you know any good leads for my project?

I was thinking that Julian and Mercy would be good prospects. Do you know any other companies?

Would you happen to know any decision makers there?

I know that the CEO, Sally Tremble, is pretty hard to reach. Can you recommend any of her direct reports?

Would you know anyone in their communications department?

I heard that their membership is pretty impressive. Who can I talk to about giving a presentation?

You may want to connect their backgrounds to your request for leads:

Since you're an expert in the field . . .

I know you've worked there for fifteen years and know the company inside and out.

As an expert in that area . . .

Since you were president of the Advertisers Association and have been on numerous boards, you're probably the most informed person around.

Be sensitive to the fact that your audience may be asked for referrals a lot or may not want to be a networking source for you. That doesn't mean you shouldn't ask: just do so cautiously:

I hope you don't mind my asking you . . .

I'm sure you get asked this a lot . . .

Since you're a known expert, I'm sure people contact you all the time about . . .

If you want to meet in person, be clear about how much time you will need:

Do you think we could meet for about half an hour next week?

I was hoping to get some information about possible clients as I build my business. It would only take an hour or two.

Do you think you can give me an hour? I'm starting up a new business and could really use your insights.

Would you mind if I dropped by your office briefly next week? It will only take fifteen minutes—tops.

It's fine to invite contacts out for a drink—but leave them some options. You don't want them to feel trapped:

I'd be happy to take you out to lunch. Or we can meet in your office.

Want to get a cup of coffee—or even better, how about a glass of wine?

I can meet you at work or somewhere after hours. Just let me know.

Would you like to do lunch?

I know a great café around the corner from you. We can go there or anywhere else you like.

If, during the discussion, you need more time, ask if your contact minds continuing. Be precise whether you'll need ten minutes or half an hour. Be sure to end the conversation then.

Would you mind staying for another twenty minutes?

It's five forty-five. Do you mind if we go until six?

What time do you need to leave?

I know I mentioned that we'd stop after twenty minutes. Can you give me another ten?

A dash of humor always helps:

I hate to be the guest who wouldn't leave, but . . .

If you give me fifteen minutes, I'll let you kick me out.

I appreciate the extra time: next time, I promise to bring a bouncer to throw me out.

Show your appreciation but avoid being trite, which will sound insincere.

Do not say:
Thank you for your time.

Thanks for being there.

I knew I could rely on you in my time of need.

I am glad you were there when I called.

Even worse than being trite, you'll sound annoying.

Do:
I really appreciate all your insights.

This was a really great meeting. I learned a lot.

Thanks so much for all that great advice. I'm planning to follow up immediately.

You've been really helpful.

Asking for Leads Indirectly

You can be indirect without being sneaky. Essentially, you're opening the door and they can step in—or not. Here are a few phrases that show how:

> *I was hoping to get in touch with someone in their senior management team.*

> *I went online but couldn't find the name of anyone in their hiring office.*

> *I'm trying to figure out who their purchasing agents are.*

> *One of the greatest mysteries is how to reach their decision makers, don't you think?*

When possible, show how that connection would be of value to you—and the person or organization you'd be contacting. This will underscore the value of your contacts' help and fuel their willingness to give you solid information:

> *If we connected, I know they'd appreciate my input.*

> *I can provide information in the presentation that will be of great value to them—even if they don't request my services.*

> *I know they'll appreciate my unusual skill set; it's exactly what they need.*

> *That group has exactly the right people for the kind of advice I can give them.*

> *If I could join Right and Sons, I think my professional goals would be met!*

> *I know they'd give me just the opportunity I need.*

If your contact hedges or says no, be polite, don't let your feelings get hurt, and leave the door open:

If you come up with any ideas, I'm always happy to hear from you.

Thanks for your honesty.

No problem. Just thought I'd ask.

I understand—these people are pretty private.

If the feeling is agreeable, ask if you can follow up:

Would you mind if I check in with you later to see if you have any ideas?

Can I update you about my progress?

Do you want me to contact you if I get through? [If so, the contact may give you names or other connections after seeing your progress.]

Asking for Leads a Second Time

Be sure to show your progress or other result from your contacts' past efforts.

When they've been helpful before:

Thank you for sending me to Tony, Roberta, and Jay. They were really helpful: I know I have traction at Cohen Brothers, thanks to you. If you have additional contacts, I'd be most appreciative.

I made lots of great contacts at the association; thanks for introducing me. Do you know of any others I can join? I know they'd be helpful.

Thanks to your introduction, I closed three deals last week. If you have any other ideas, please let me know!

When they haven't helped before but told you to get in touch later:

It's hard to believe two months have passed since we spoke last. So, I'm getting in touch about my progress and to see if you have any thoughts to pass along.

When we met at your office, you mentioned that you may have some names you could pass along. Just checking in to see if you have them.

I'd really appreciate getting any ideas from you as I continue to progress in my job search.

You don't have to ask them for a lead—just updating them might be enough:

In our conversation last month, you said you'd be interested in hearing about my progress.

After our meeting in January, I learned some interesting news about the future of XCV. Perhaps we can talk?

When we met in New York, I mentioned that I was hoping to secure two new sales positions. Since then, I . . .

Use "forward-sounding" words when discussing your activity. This will invigorate the conversation and help your contacts feel as if they are dealing with a winner. Forward-sounding words include:

Progress

Move forward

Move ahead

Advancing

Going along

Heading forward

Growing

Developing

When possible, offer something in return:

After the networking meeting last week, I had some interesting conversations with people from the bank. Would you like me to send them your way?

I haven't forgotten that I promised to assess your business plan. Let me know when you're ready.

I'd like to celebrate my progress so far. Would you care to join me for lunch or a drink?

Would you like a case of our new variety? We just got them in and I'd like to send some along. [Only for a networking partner—not if you're applying for a job or trying to generate sales. This might seem like a bribe.]

I'd like to send you that book I mentioned last week. What is the best address?

Letting Them Know When a Lead Is Not Appropriate (Without Sounding Ungrateful)

Don't waste their time, or yours, by having your contacts provide useless information. But—don't insult them either. Instead, show appreciation, then gently steer them in the right direction. Use words that indicate appreciation:

Appreciate

Grateful

Glad

Thanks

Use phrases like these:

I appreciate your insights. I also need to know about the Consumer Relations Department. Do you have any information about them?

Thanks for your leads. They sound like helpful people. Would you also happen to know someone in research?

I think the most direct route would be to speak with a senior VP. Do you know anyone in that area?

I was hoping to meet with Sean Elliot, also. Do you know anything about him?

The Kennel Club is a great idea. I was thinking, though, that I might try contacting Kitty Kats, Inc. What do you think about them?

Asking for Leads That You Would Otherwise Have to Pay For

Make sure you—and your contacts—know your search is aboveboard and you're not a nuisance caller or spammer.

Would you happen to have names of contacts in . . .

I know that a list is pretty expensive, and I don't have the cash flow right now. Do you know alternate ways of getting the information?

I tried finding the names online, but it's a slow process. Do you have any ideas of how I can find them without paying a fortune?

Could you send along any lists of organizations and the department heads? If so, then I'll send you what I have and we should create a master list.

Getting Inside Information

You can be direct—as the old saying goes: "No harm in asking."

Do you know the CEO of that company?

Who's the guy in charge of acquisitions?

Would you happen to know who makes the hiring decision? The website says it's Sheila Butler, but she moved on months ago.

Do you know who Don Connolly's replacement is?

How many of the top brass were laid off? Do you know any of their replacements?

Do you mind if I ask you a few questions about your company?

I'm trying to figure out the best way to approach the decision makers. Do you have any advice?

Do you know what they're specifically interested in hearing about?

What problems are they trying to solve?

If you have more than one or two pieces of information you're hoping to receive, tell your contacts how many. This will create a framework for the interaction and prevent them from feeling overwhelmed. Use specific numbers or general terms like "a few":

I had a few questions I was hoping you could address.

Would you mind answering five short questions?

I'd like to ask you three or four questions about the best way to reach people at the company. Is that OK?

I was hoping you could answer two questions.

Be clear that you're not asking them to reveal secrets or trying to get competitive knowledge. While *you* may know that honesty is the best policy, they may misinterpret your request. Clarity about honesty is best:

I want to be clear, I'm only asking for information that's appropriate for the public.

Please let me know if I'm asking inappropriate questions.

I'm not trying to get privileged information.

As I'm sure you know, I'm not trying to do anything unethical. I am just trying to get insights that will help me navigate the company a little better.

Don't assume that a senior-level person is a man. Plenty of women rocket up the ranks and will be offended if you address them as "he." Similarly, the person you're networking with might think you're naive or ill-informed if you immediately assume the person in charge is a man.

Chapter 4

Following Up

In marketing, there's a saying: "love at fifth sight." That means it takes five attempts (or more) for someone to respond to your message. In many ways, networking is much like marketing (or, as you'll see later in this book, marketing is actually a form of networking!). You must follow up once or twice to ensure your contacts give you the names or other information they promised. And, you must keep following up now and then to ensure they remember you when additional leads crop up.

One other saying that's critical to remember as we move forward: "timing is everything." Yes, you need to follow up—but when? Too soon and you'll seem to be nagging. Wait too long and they may forget you. Instead, you must find that comfort zone for your contacts. Are they busy? (Most likely, yes.) Do they travel a lot? Have lots of commitments? Is there a pressing matter, such as an upcoming conference or new developments in your field that will give you good reason to contact them?

Finally, what's the best way to get in touch? By telephone? E-mail? And what do you hope to get from them? If it's a name and number, e-mail may work best. If you want to connect on a personal level, maybe brainstorm, then pick up the phone. As for social networks? Blogs? These are significant opportunities but slightly more complex.

Keep them in the back of your mind for now: we'll address them in greater detail in other sections of this book.

Determining When to Follow Up

So, you met with the contact or had a conversation on the phone. That person was helpful but didn't have the information you needed. She said something like: "Get in touch with me later." Or, "Let me see if I can get you that contact information." All was well and good, but pretty nebulous. When should you get back in touch? And how? Rather than guess and hope for the best, you should find out.

First, determine the time and day that works best for your contact—this is pretty straightforward:

When should I follow up?

What's the best time for me to get in touch?

When should I contact you?

If she doesn't respond right away, you can recommend a date:

Does the seventeenth work for you?

Would you like me to call on a Monday?

I can call you again in mid-July. Does that sound good?

When would you like me to get in touch? Next month?

Be sure to get her to agree to the follow-up time, if not outright suggest it. That way, when you follow up, you can say things like: "As you suggested, I'm following up today," or "When we last talked, you recommended that I contact you today." A lightbulb goes off, she remembers, and she's more likely to pay attention. Here's what you can say:

Which time is best for you? Two o'clock? How about three o'clock?

Which week is best—the first or second of November?

What time is best for you? Early in the morning? Oh, good, does eight or nine work better for you?

Also, check in about the best way to reach her. Some people prefer phone calls; others like e-mails:

Would you like me to e-mail you or call?

What is the best way to reach you?

I can e-mail, call, or whatever else works best for you.

If you got along famously well, you may want to suggest going out for lunch or a cup of coffee the next time around:

Want to get lunch at the Grille next time?

Maybe we can get a bite to eat the next time we get together.

Want to go to the Alston Grille? I heard the food is great.

We can meet at Starbucks, if you like.

If you're not too busy, maybe we can go out for a coffee or afternoon drink. [Drinks work well with some contacts and not so well with others. Use your judgment on this one.]

Meeting for dinner can create a stronger and more rewarding bond, but it does take time. So, be sure to give your contact an out:

Maybe we can get a bite to eat.

If you want to meet later in the day, we can always go to Shep's Café for dinner.

43

Will you be hungry after work?

We could always get a light dinner, have a chance to talk, and avoid the rush-hour traffic home.

You can offer to treat your contact, just make sure the situation won't lead him to believe you're trying to bribe him. Keep the language relaxed and friendly and avoid words like "pay" or "buy":

Do not:
Can I buy you dinner?

I want to pay the bill next time. Will that be all right?

I want to buy you a meal.

I'll pay for the drinks and dinner.

Do:
Can I treat you to a bite next time?

Next time, lunch is on me.

Next time, I hope you let me foot the bill.

Avoid words that suggest an hours-long affair and will inspire the busy contact to say no:

Do not:
An evening out

Go out to eat

Go to a restaurant

Have supper

Get dinner and drinks

Dine out

Do:

Get a bite to eat after work

Have a drink

Have a light dinner

Get something to eat after work

Or name a place that provides quick service for short rendezvous:

Want to go to Chelsea's?

Maybe we can meet at Ron and Elvin's.

*If you want a little fresh air, we can always go to Conrad's.
They have tables outside.*

If you're not absolutely sure the answer is yes, don't invite the contact out on the phone: this may put him in an awkward position if he wants to say no. Instead, e-mail him. Make your e-mail invitations open-ended:

I can meet you wherever you like: in your office or at Chelsea's across the street.

Where is the best place for us to meet?

Do you want a break or should we meet in your office?

Pointer: In-person meet-ups are always best when you're first getting together with someone. The experience is deeper, more positive, and more enduring. Subsequent meetings can be in person or by e-mail, although even here, in person is best.

Following Up Immediately After Your Request

The immediate follow-up should be by e-mail. This will give your contacts space: if they want to read it they will. If not, no problem. Be sure to acknowledge your meeting but be specific and sincere. Create an honest thanks:

Do not:
Thank you for your time last week.

I enjoyed meeting with you last week.

Thank you for taking the time to meet with me last Monday.

Thank you for talking to me last week.

I appreciate your taking time from your busy schedule to meet with me on Friday.

Instead, find something you really did value about the meeting and go from there:

Thanks for treating me to lunch last week.

I really appreciate all your insights into the Marble Corporation.

I had a great time having lunch with you last week; I never knew waitstaff could be so spunky!

Many thanks for taking the steps involved in getting contracts from the ADCB.

Thank you for your insights into TellTalk.

Should you use "thanks" or "thank you"? Depends on the person. A younger person, accustomed to the informal language of Blackberries, e-mails, and social networks will feel fine about a quick "thanks." A boomer, someone with a formal style, or those who take themselves seriously will respond better to "thank you." Keep the rest of your message consistently formal or informal. Then, show your contact how you'll use the information he or she presented:

I'll get back to the folks on your team early next week.

I definitely will join the social network, as you suggested.

I'm planning to send everyone you mentioned a link to my blog. I agree, they may be interested in commenting.

I'll call Lonnie Latzig tomorrow. I think he will be incredibly helpful.

Here are two exceptions to the e-mailing-your-thanks rule: when they asked you to send something or they suggested that you call. When you're sending something, whether through the post or an e-mail, then it's OK to call to ensure that they got it. If they are too busy to answer, leave a message on their voice mail or with their assistant:

I'm checking in to make sure you received the books I sent last week.

Since I didn't hear back from you, I'm calling to make sure you received my e-mail and the attachment.

Just calling to say hello and make sure you received the package.

I was concerned that my package may have been stuck in security. I wrote "Books" on the package as you suggested, but I wanted to check anyway.

If the person suggested that you call, then you can push harder. You can say:

I'm calling, as you suggested last week.

Just giving you a call, as I promised.

If an assistant takes the message, make sure that person knows the contact wanted you to call and you're expected:

Tony asked me to call him today.

I'm calling him about a meeting we had. He asked me to follow up.

I'm trying to reach Marcia—she suggested I give her a ring.

If the contact isn't in, persist:

Do you know when I can reach her?

Should I call back in an hour?

When's a good time to try back?

Can you recommend when I can call?

Whatever else you do, don't leave it up to your contacts to call you. They're taking the call for your benefit—not theirs. That means you don't want to give them an additional task and they probably won't call anyway, since you won't be at the top of their overly crowded to-do list (nothing personal).

Several Weeks After the Initial Contact

Following up a week or two or longer after an initial meeting can be more demanding than immediately after. Does your contact remember you? If he was enthusiastic, will the energy have endured? You need to recharge his enthusiasm, remind him of your discussion, and convince him to pass on leads, invitations, or information, all discreetly, of course.

Remind him of your last contact—but don't be obvious:

Do not:
I don't know if you remember me but . . .

I met you in your office on . . .

I was referred to you by April Sun and we had lunch in the cafeteria.

You may not remember me but . . .

Probably you don't know who I am . . .

Instead, build in the reminder:

I hope you've been well since our lunch.

I just saw April Sun today and let her know we met last month. She sends her regards.

I hope things have calmed down at the office—although a busy office is usually a productive one.

Since we met last month, many exciting changes have occurred.

Then tell him how you followed up with his suggestions:

I signed up for the free newsletters online, as you recommended. They're really helpful!

I contacted your associate, Mike, at Pond Ice. He gave me really great information.

I contacted everyone on your list immediately after you sent it. I now have some really great prospects.

After we spoke, I joined the Garment Makers Association, as you suggested. I'll be attending their spring conference on imports.

If something definite came as a result of his suggestions—don't wait! Contact him immediately:

Wanted you to know my good news! Thanks to your referral to Thomas Benson and Sheila McCray I just won two contracts.

Wanted you to be the first to know—I'm going for an interview at Close CPA next week. Thanks for the referral. I'll let you know what happens.

Well—I landed the speaking gig at the USMC. Thanks so much for suggesting it, and for all your insights on how to present my talk!

Just got the news: I am meeting the next CMO at InterCom. Thank you, thank you, thank you!

Don't be afraid to let your enthusiasm show. Your contacts gave you valuable leads or other information. Let them share in the payoff.

Offer a celebratory drink or lunch, when appropriate. This will help cement the relationship and possibly lead to professional relationships. Just be sure your contacts know this is a friendly, and not romantic, gesture! Some appropriate invitations include:

Would you like to get a glass of wine so I can thank you for the lead?

Why don't you join my assistant and me to celebrate the new contract?

Want to go out for lunch on Friday? We can go to the Chamber Club. It's right near your office!

I'm having a get-together at the office to celebrate. Would you like to join us?

If you're actually requesting more connections, ask for what you need—be polite and not demanding:

Do not:
I'd like you to send me more names, as the ones you gave me were updated.

Please call me today or tomorrow to advise me about next steps.

Call me tomorrow so I can update you.

I need to know the name of the CEO at the Lang Group, Teller's Trust, and the Wildlife Society. Please send them as soon as possible.

Time is short—please contact me tomorrow.

Do:
Do you think we could talk later today or tomorrow? Your ideas last month were helpful and I'd like to chat with you further.

I was hoping you knew where I could find an updated list. Things change so quickly these days, many of the folks you mentioned have moved on or retired!

I was hoping you could give me insights into a few more prospects.

Since we last spoke, we're trying to reach out to donors with interest in environmental concerns. Would you have any ideas?

People love to help, so don't shy away from using the word:

Could you help me determine the right department?

I was hoping to get some help in finding the best ways to reach the senior staff. Could you give me some advice?

Your help was invaluable last month. I was hoping you could provide more insight.

When the Contact Didn't Follow Through with a Promise

Let's face it: your contacts *are* doing you a favor. And they are putting their reputations on the line, should you use their name. So, you can't exactly force them to follow through. But they *did* promise. And you *do* need the help. Here's what you do: send a reminder, assuming they forgot. Start with a personal note:

Hope you've been well since our lunch at the Yellow Brick Bank.

Hope you weren't stuck in the snowstorm yesterday. What a mess!

Just checking in since our last get-together. How's your cold?

After the conference I was stuck at the airport for six hours. Makes you realize the truth behind the saying "There's no place like home."

I heard from Jacob, who was at the networking meeting. You remember him, right? With the bow tie? Seems he landed the much-coveted editor-in-chief position at Redwall Books. Can you imagine!

Then remind them:

Anyway, could you send along that list we discussed?

Do you have any time to send me the contact information?

Could you send along the names of the folks at the PR Forum?

I'm hoping to contact the folks at Arbitron tomorrow. Could you send along those names?

Be friendly—put away anger, frustration, or guilt.

Do not:
As you know, I'm looking for a job in a tough economy. This isn't exactly easy, and you said you would help.

I'm waiting to hear from you. You said you'd get back to me this week. It's Friday—and nothing.

Can you please call me, as you said you would?

It's really important to keep promises. Would you please keep yours?

Update them about your progress, then ask for the follow-up:

Since we met, I've been attending networking groups every week. Phew! Lots of work, but enjoyable. No one seems to know about the contacts you mentioned. Could you send those names along?

So far, I've had two interviews and they both look promising. Do you think you could send along the information about Weatherford? I'd like to contact them as well.

Since we talked, I've been in four states and six cities. And I'm ready to go to more! Could you send me those contacts for the Bay Area? Seems like a great next step.

Show that you're especially ready and explain why you need their information:

I met with Julia Michaels. She's really fascinating and speaks highly of you. Do you happen to have Jean's number? She's next on my list.

I have an appointment with the senior vice president of Human Resources next week. Think I could call Veronica, as you recommended? I'm sure she'll have some great advice.

I'm going to Massachusetts on Friday. Could you get me those numbers, by any chance? I'd like to set up some meetings when I'm there.

When the Contact Sent You to the Wrong Person

Be delicate here. You don't want your contact to feel out of touch or foolish. But you do want him to get you the right name.

I tried contacting Wayne Johnson, but he isn't at the company anymore. Would you happen to know his replacement?

Big news from the City Group. Seems they sold off the entire communications department. So, Betty Jordan is no longer there. Do you have a better contact person, instead?

Thanks so much for connecting me to Fred Wilson. He e-mailed me and is actually working in IT. He recommended I ask you for someone in their data-processing department. Do you know anyone else?

I tried e-mailing Jerry Webber, but my message kept bouncing back. Could you confirm that I have the right spelling?

Take a light approach when you're on a familiar basis with the contact:

Turns out no Mary Wilson works at Fallstaff. Maybe she retired? Anyway, do you know anyone else?

I called the Atom Group. The secretary kept saying "who?" until I got the picture. No one by the name of Betty Ford. She seemed to think I meant the former first lady.

Turns out Atkins Technical never heard of Morrie Stein. Maybe it's a virtual presence? Anyway, do you have another contact name?

Do not use negative or slightly accusatory words. Stay away from the following:

Wrong name

Incorrect

Inaccurate

Bogus

Antiquated

Outdated

Bad

Useless

Futile

Inadequate

Worthless

Unhelpful

When the Contact Agreed to Approach Someone on Your Behalf

Usually, contacts will "cc" you or otherwise let you know if they made the connection. If this didn't happen, then follow up, just to make sure:

Just checking in to see if you reached Harry Schindler. If so, I'll give him a call.

I was planning to call Don Chase at the bank next week. But I wanted to make sure you had been able to contact him first.

When we talked on Monday, you said you'd contact Jane by midweek. Just checking before I e-mailed her.

Thanks for getting in touch with Dr. Pointer at the Neighborhood Clinic. I'm planning to call him tomorrow, unless you say otherwise.

Thanks for offering to contact Mr. Robins. Were you able to reach him? If so, I'll shoot him an e-mail.

You can let your contacts know your plans. This will validate the fact that they made the connection or will put low-level pressure if they didn't:

I was going to call Kenneth Frank next week when I'll be on the West Coast. Were you able to get in touch? If not, I won't call.

The deadline for the proposal is coming up. OK if I call Dr. Grant today or tomorrow?

We were hoping to reach targets in three areas: sales, marketing, and general communications. And—thanks to you—we have great contacts in all areas. So, we're going to call them next week, unless you say otherwise.

What do you do when the third party didn't hear from your contact? Embarrassing, right? Actually, this can be embarrassing for everyone involved. So, let your contact know what happened, too. Be quick and easy:

Just a quick heads-up: I contacted Kevin at the ARET on Wednesday. He never got the e-mail you sent him. So, I let him know how we met and why you thought we should get in touch.

When we spoke, you mentioned that you would call Todd's administrative assistant to set up an interview with him. She said she never heard from you and will wait to get an e-mail. Can you let me know when you have a chance to send it out?

Just wanted you to know that I contacted your managers about the Pro-Products we provide, as you recommended in your last e-mail. I called Gerry Gibbons in Kansas and Kelly Reilly in Utah. Neither one heard from you in advance though, so I'll hold off.

Humor never hurts:

Oops! I contacted the folks in Alpha-Bet and they never got your message.

I know people call me speedy, but I definitely went too fast this time! I sent the folks on your list an e-mail mentioning your endorsement. I heard from a few of them saying they never got your introduction. Sorry about that!

Hmm . . . Did I jump the gun? I contacted Keller and Fay yesterday.

Chapter 5

Cold Contacts

In the best of all worlds, every contact you made in the networking universe would be with people you knew personally. People who respected if not actually loved you. But unfortunately, that world would be very small, so most of your contacts will be cold.

To keep them from being icy, however, you need to make them as personal as possible. You can do this in a number of ways, which we'll explore in detail in this chapter. Here is a quick overview:

- Personalize the first line or the first few sentences of your correspondence. This will establish a friendly connection. Don't have a personal tidbit? Find one. Go online, ask around, do anything you can or don't bother making the connection.
- Never, ever use a canned opening. It will be a real stopper. Enough said.
- Ask questions. These have an engaging quality that can break through the coolness of addressing strangers.

Finally, you need to relax when contacting unknowns. Otherwise, you might inadvertently be stiff, distant, or awkward, and detract from the potential of your communication.

When You Heard About the Person Directly

This is relatively easy. However you heard about these contacts—and whatever you heard them say—was probably positive. Otherwise, you wouldn't be contacting them, right? Be sure to use specifics so they know you're authentic.

Do not:

I am writing in order to . . .

This is an inquiry about . . .

I am hoping to learn more about your organization, which I learned about in . . .

The reason for this e-mail is . . .

Can you please give me information about . . .

Do:

I've heard about your product from the folks at the Rotary Club on West Fifteenth Street. They speak highly of your service—twenty-four hours is pretty quick! So, I wanted to get in touch.

Several years ago, you met with a friend of mine, Laura Sparks. She speaks highly of you and recommended that we connect.

I just moved to New York City and have been looking for a work environment that would enable me to contribute on many levels. My friend Jane Hersh worked for you for almost ten years, until she had a baby, and she thinks the fit is great.

We met at Janice Simpson's retirement party last year. We had a great talk about the new developments in Landmark Park.

Rely on objective information about them:

. . . the highest employee record of any small business in the three-state region.

. . . profits are consistently high, even in a troubled economy.

. . . amazing write-ups in the **Standard Daily***.*

. . . ongoing commendations throughout the ten years that I've lived in the area.

Avoid syrupy, fawning, or overly complimentary words such as these:

Stellar reputation

A leader in the industry

A proven track record

An outstanding reputation

The best in the field

An amazing reputation

A remarkable success rate

They sound insincere—even phony.

Of course, in some situations, you may have heard negative things such as the organization was falling apart, the employees were leaving in droves, or the profits were wiping away. They need your service. Your expertise. But how do you say this politely? Be clear about why you're contacting them, but don't box yourself in, just in case:

I'm a communications expert and was interested in your current situation.

I understand that you will be searching for a new CFO now that Mr. Benson and his staff have left the company.

Since you are going through a major layoff, I thought you could use assistance in . . .

Be sure to say something positive. But keep it real. Why are you contacting them, aside from their recent troubles? As always, be specific:

I know that a company that's 100 years old, as yours is, can overcome obstacles. I'd like to participate as a contractor or employee.

Given your reputation as the first organization to successfully . . .

Your history of sponsoring such programs as _____ ensures that you will recover quickly.

While I know this is the best possible move, I can help you explore best practices so you will experience success.

Show the link between you and them:

I have helped more than fifty companies in situations like yours find success.

Throughout my twenty-five years as an HR consultant, I have addressed issues like these for otherwise successful corporations such as . . .

I have conducted research for the U.S. government, Research International, and other organizations. I'm certain my insights will be of value to you.

As the former CIO of Yahooey, I can provide invaluable insights or even lead your team until you find a full-time replacement.

If the person you reached isn't the right contact, ask for the name of someone who can help:

Could you let me know the right person to talk to?

Who should I contact to discuss this matter further?

I was wondering who the best person was to speak to in the accounting department.

Should I contact your personnel office? Or your HR department? And, who would be the best person to reach?

Can you recommend someone for me to talk to?

When you contact that person, be sure to mention your original contact's name. When appropriate, mention his or her title:

Marcia Stepford, in HR, passed your name along.

Devin Foley, the company's operations manager, suggested that I contact you.

I got your address from Patricia Riley in Sales.

Elvin Harris, Gert Harris's grandson, thought we should talk.

If you were referred by a lower-level employee, you may want to mention the office he or she came from if the business is large. Otherwise, your contact may not know the person who originally sent you:

The folks in the CEO's office said to contact you.

I got your name from HR.

The PR and marketing departments passed along your contact information.

If the organization is small, go ahead and mention the contact by name. Then ask for a meeting:

> *Do you think we could meet for a short time to discuss opportunities?*
>
> *I'd like to share my experience and ideas. Do you have any time at the end of the week?*
>
> *Would you be available to meet next Friday?*
>
> *Do you want to meet and discuss our findings? I'm certain you'll find them interesting.*

Try to be specific about when you can meet—and a reason why:

> *I'll be in town next Wednesday. Would we be able to meet then?*
>
> *I'm giving a talk at the Convention Center on July 13. Do you think we can meet then?*
>
> *My article on companies in positions like yours will be out in this week's* Time Studies. *Would you like to discuss it then?*

The more impressive—and professional—the better. But you can mention family matters, provided that you *just* mention them. No detail. No stories. And no complaining.

No, no, no:
I'll be coming to town next week to help my 91-year-old mother move to a nursing home. She doesn't want to go, so, as you can imagine, it's a nightmare for all of us.

I went bankrupt several years ago and need to straighten things up. So, I will be at my lawyer's office on Tuesday afternoon. Can I see you earlier that day?

I've been really depressed these days. And your town happens to be the one place that makes me feel good. Perhaps we can meet when I'm there?

It's always best to send an e-mail first, then follow up with a phone call. Among other things, this gives you reason to talk:

I was calling to see if you received my e-mail.

I e-mailed her last week and was following up. Is she available?

I'm following up on an e-mail I sent on Tuesday.

All the better if you included an attachment of an interesting article or some other valuable item. For example, if you published an article or have a quality blog with information your contact would appreciate, discuss that. But don't bother mentioning a bio, marketing piece, résumé, or other attachment. Here's what you say:

I sent along an article I just published in International Relations Today. *The content related to your current situation; I thought you might want to discuss it.*

I was hoping to talk to Dr. Franklin to see if he received a fact sheet I thought he'd find interesting.

You Know the Person by Reputation

When you have a history with your contacts:

I have eaten crepes at your restaurant since I was a kid in Milwaukee. So, when I was thinking of where I'd most like to work as I begin my profession in culinary management, I immediately thought of you.

I was hoping to get information about the best person to speak with about our services. Since I've been a customer at your facility for almost twenty years, I know the level of service you provide and would like to be part of it.

My father, Harold Jones, and my uncle, Fred Hawkins, both worked at your firm for many years. Their branch has since relocated, but I'd like to know about employment opportunities and keep our family in your employee base!

When they win awards:

I read about the award you received for optimal customer service. This inspired me to contact you and see about opportunities to be part of your team.

Congratulations on the City Award for Excellence—again! After hearing so much about your company, I was eager to discuss areas where our services overlap.

They're generous to the community:

I've come to know your organization well through my work with your volunteer employees for the Stone Soup Community Center. I was hoping I could meet with someone in your outreach program to let you know about some other valuable projects.

Over the past ten years, my son has been playing for your company's soccer league. So, I feel like I'm part of your team. I was hoping to talk to someone there about making it more official (and professional) by discussing opportunities for employees or contractors in your IT department.

They're popular or otherwise well known in the field:

Your work in pea-pod research is renowned, and I was hoping I could meet with someone there to discuss how I might contribute.

I've been following your growth since you were a small partnership in Inman Square, and I have been impressed with your unique approaches. I remember when you first announced . . .

Your success in winning three tournaments has impressed all of us at . . .

You must be specific about what impresses you most. Otherwise, your views might appear as idle chatter. Notice the difference:

Do not:
Your company has an amazing reputation for innovation.

You are most certainly a leader in your field.

Your customer service record is well known.

Do:
Your innovative approaches, including your Disc Recovery System, have made amazing changes in the industry.

Since your company has been number one for sixteen years . . .

One reason I was interested in contacting you was your record in customer service: being voted the number one best company by employees for three consecutive years is impressive.

Then, tell them something about yourself. Be specific and make sure it reflects a quality of your experience and expertise that will impress them most. For example:

I read about the award you received for optimal customer service. . . . I led the team at Spencer's that won notoriety for its groundbreaking customer service techniques.

I've come to know your organization well through my work with your volunteer employees for the Stone Soup Community Center. Many of our programs overlap with the ones you currently participate in and won't require additional employee time.

Your work in pea-pod research is renowned. I was involved in the soybean studies that won much publicity in 1994.

Finally, get a commitment from them to move to the next step in your discussion. A meeting? Another contact for you to reach? Either way, seal the next part of the deal right then and keep moving.

In networking, your point in reaching the expert is to get leads, ideas, and insights that will take you in the direction you most want to go. This is significantly different from sales calls or other marketing initiatives where your objective is to make a sale. Therefore, be clear about your motivations. Remember, people are usually happy to dispense advice. It compliments them and gives them the satisfaction of helping you.

Here's what you should say at the start of the conversation or written message:

I'm not calling to pitch anything, just so you know. But I would greatly appreciate some insights as I move forward.

I'd like to meet with you for informational purposes only.

I was hoping you could give me advice. Is that OK?

Do you think you could give me some insights?

Can you give me some advice about this field?

Be sure to put a time limit on your discussion:

I promise to stay for only fifteen minutes.

This will only take ten minutes on the phone.

Our phone call will only go for about fifteen minutes—until ten fifteen, no later.

Or mention the number of questions you would want to ask:

I was hoping you could answer two questions.

I have three quick questions I was hoping you could address.

You Read About the Person or Organization in a Publication

Contacting people or organizations that you know from a publication by or about them is always a good thing. For example, if you read about them in a trade magazine or journal, it shows that (1) you're informed; (2) you're intelligent, since you read and possibly research issues within your industry; (3) you like their thinking given whatever they discussed in the article; (4) you're part of their club (as demonstrated by the fact that you read publications like-minded people enjoy); and (5) you'll contribute to their organization in a meaningful way.

The first question you should ask is this: should you e-mail or mail the message? This is slightly harder to answer as you want your communication to have a personal quality to it. The answer comes down to this: what would your audience most appreciate? If you read a way-cool article about skateboarding, e-mail. Text message. Do whatever.

If you read a serious piece on some scientific formulation in an established trade journal, go postal. And, if you're contacting a CEO, CFO, CIO—you get the idea—a senior-level person with an administrative assistant, a card might work well. It could get you past the gatekeepers and, even better, give you a reason to chat with him or her when you call. Quick perfect phrase example: "I was wondering if he got my card." Of course, the card must be tasteful and memorable. No cute puppies allowed!

Warning: Every time I've made a big splash in the media, such as an article about my ideas or business, or a cool appearance on a Big Medium, such as TV, I get these types of messages from perfect strangers:

> *Congratulations! I saw you were featured on* **Professional Person's Magazine.**
>
> *Wow—great. You got all the publicity anyone would want. What's your secret?*
>
> *Amazing.*
>
> *Good!*
>
> *Fabulous—Jeff Starr featured you in his blog!*

OK, so what's wrong with these comments? They're beside the point. The media exposure isn't about getting attention, it's about the content. And what if I've actually had more and better exposure? Is this "congratulations" necessary? Rather, it's a wee bit condescending. This big break was actually one of many breaks that were nice but not like getting, say, a huge check.

Instead, they could have personalized the message, drawn a clear connection, and demonstrated how the synergy was there. Here are some ideas of what they could have said—and you *should* say—when contacting someone you meet in online or off-line print:

Introducing the Article or Publication

Be specific even here. State the publication and date. If the publication has a familiar nickname, use that. It shows you're part of the crowd, so to speak:

> *I read your article in* **Physician's Times** *last month.*

> *I saw your quote about the use of steroids in this week's edition of* **Men's Health** *and found your insights quite unusual and refreshing.*

> *I read the interview you did with Anne Benoit in the February edition of* **Modern Men's Thinking** *and found it of great interest for many reasons.*

> *Interesting interview with Stan Weinburg in this month's* **Journalism Review!**

If you're an expert in the field or have notoriety in some way, definitely mention that first. If you have been involved in that field or are interested in it, save the relationship issue for the next sentence:

> *As a former consultant to the CEO of Enormous Corporation, I found your article about organizational downsizing to be of immense interest.*

> *For the last ten years, I have been the team lead on data management reengineering at Booz Allen. So, you can imagine how interested I was to read your perspective in* **The Data Journal** *last month.*

> *For twenty-five years, I was a senior manager in Web Company, which you discussed in your white paper on the Connections.com website.*

And wouldn't this be nice:

You quoted me at length about the difference between cost analysis models in your article in **Financial Matters**.

Do not use general terms to describe yourself—you will sound more like you're bragging and less like you're authentic:

Do not:
I am an expert at . . .

As a known leader in . . .

As the foremost authority on . . .

Most people agree that I am among the top knowledge holders in . . .

As one of the founders of . . .

Instead, provide objective and reliable specifics that will open doors whether online or on the phone.

Next, state what interested you most about the piece—whether it's something they were quoted as saying or something they wrote. Be specific about what interested you (of course) without providing boring or otherwise unnecessary detail.

Here are examples of specifics; obviously yours will depend on the subject matter:

Your approach to caring for immigrant children in a hospital setting was revolutionary and raises critical interest in this matter.

As a men's health professional, I was interested in how men can actually apply your ideas not only for a few days or weeks, but consistently.

Your insights proved that the old models are working much more than anyone thought and need tweaking but not an entire overhaul.

It's always great to see excitement and optimism in an otherwise dismal field.

Do not go into detail about your point of view—they probably don't care unless you're a reigning expert in that field. Instead, summarize.

Do not:
I agree with your position for the following ten reasons, as I've indicated below.

I have enclosed a three-page rebuttal to your critics' opinions plus some biographical information about me.

Having been engaged in research in that area for two decades, I thought you would appreciate additional insights. So, I have attached several of my research findings, including comments I received from peers, and related articles.

Do:
I agree with your position for a number of reasons. Most significant is that you . . .

I have found many flaws in your critics' comments, which I have published at www.commentsaboutthings.com.

Having been engaged in research in that area for two decades, I found that your viewpoints were both valid and instructive.

Shifting to Your Interests

Be sure to draw a connection to the point you immediately made and not interject a new point suddenly:

From: *I agree with your position for a number of reasons. Most significant is that you . . .*

To: *I would like to discuss these with you for ten or fifteen minutes next week. Is that possible?*

From: *I have found many flaws in your critics' comments, which I have published at www.commentsaboutthings.com.*

To: *If you like, I can send these to you and perhaps follow up with a quick phone call.*

Signing off:
Please let me know what time works for you.

What time is best for you?

Does Monday from ten to ten thirty sound good?

Would you be available for a brief chat on Monday, Wednesday, or Friday of next week?

I will be in the Claremont area next week. Would you be available to talk for a short time?

You Heard the Person on a Webinar or Other Talk

As always, set a context. When did you hear your prospective contact give the talk? What did you like most about it?

> *I participated in CareerGrowers Webinar on April 14 and was most impressed with your insights into how to reach senior-level executives.*

> *As a participant in the Sales Rep Conference in May, I was most impressed with your session on how to network from the bottom up.*

If you have experience or background that would interest her, mention that. Then make future plans:

I was hoping to chat with you about your ideas, if that's all right.

Would you be available to talk on Wednesday morning?

Be aware that many professionals who give talks, whether online or in person, do so as a networking opportunity for themselves. They are unlikely to dispense information for free when they get paid to do it as a consultant. This doesn't mean that you shouldn't contact them as a networking opportunity. But do be aware of their professional motivations. Here are some phrases that can help:

I understand that you are a professional consultant, and I will not take advantage of your time.

I do recognize that you are a professional and will only ask you a few questions, if that's OK.

Ideally, of course, you will be able to pay a consulting fee either at that point or sometime in the near future. If so, let the contact know this:

I spoke with my boss and she agreed that we may want your services in the near future. For now, though, I was hoping you could answer a few questions.

Our training department frequently brings in professionals like you to give talks or train our employees. While I just need a small amount of feedback, I have contacted them about bringing you in for a full session.

I spoke with the events planning committee of the association and recommended that they speak to you about giving a talk. For now, though, I was hoping you could answer a few questions. Is that all right?

Please let me know if we can speak briefly next week. At that time, I'll also pass along the names of our training staff and their contact information. They may be interested in having you in as a speaker.

Be honest! It's wrong to mislead! If you cannot offer the person an opportunity to get paid work, think about offering something else. In other words, you become the networking contact as well:

I'd be happy to give you any leads that will help you get additional training—you were quite good.

Please let me know if I can return the favor.

After spending the last twenty years in this company, I may be able to give you insights about how to reach people here, if you like.

For many years, I was president of the Soap and Perfume Makers Association. Please let me know if I can give you any useful information based on this experience.

Would you like me to send you some lists that will help you find speaking opportunities?

I would be happy to arrange a meeting between you and people in our training department. Just let me know.

You Found the Person in the Blogosphere

We'll discuss networking online later in this book. But cold calls through blogs do merit a bit of attention now, too.

First, let the contact know that you enjoy his blog and, when helpful, why:

I've been reading your blog for over a year. Your insights into the publishing universe are really amazing.

A friend sent me a link to your blog about two years ago. I've been a regular ever since.

I signed up for your newsletter through your blog several months ago. I was especially riveted by your insights into learning styles that was in this week's edition.

Be direct and let him know what you want:

I was hoping to get some information from you about the publishers you found most approachable for authors who don't have an agent. Would you be able to share that with me?

I wanted to reach several of the groups that have links on your site but wasn't sure of the best approach. Would you mind talking later this week?

Since you're an expert in parenting, I wondered if you knew any groups that have innovative approaches.

Should you e-mail bloggers through their site or call them on the phone? That depends. If the blogger has a phone number on the site, go ahead and call. Or, e-mail and ask if you can call on a specific date. The number tells you something about the blogger's comfort level with phone calls, even from strangers. However, if the only way to reach the blogger is through the site, that will have to do. You can always ask for a phone or face-to-face discussion, but don't push the issue.

Chapter 6

Getting New Leads from an Old Contact

Getting leads and other information from old contacts is a good deal. You know them already. You have memories and common interests that can open your discussion. And, you have a rhythm to your relationships: you know whether to reach them by e-mail or phone call, what to expect for timing, and what they may appreciate in return.

Do be sure to strike a balance, though. If you just got some hot leads from a contact, give her a little space. Pace your interactions. And express your gratitude appropriately. A thank-you now and then is one thing. Lunch out is better. My opinion: a beer and really cool snacks after work is best. But that would depend on your contact.

When the Previous Leads Worked Out

Let your contact know about the success immediately afterward. An e-mail is good but a phone call can be better:

> *I just heard from the Hotchkins Group. They offered us a five-year contract to handle all their accounting! Thank you, thank you, thank you!*

I spoke to Mr. Fitzpatrick, as you recommended, and he put me directly in touch with his sales manager. I know your good word got him to act so promptly.

Guess what! I've been invited to be the keynote speaker at the ASB Award ceremony. Many thanks for sending me to Patty and for putting in a good word. Think you'll be there?

A celebratory drink or dinner? Possibly, depending on the magnitude of the rewards from their efforts. Either way, give your contacts a choice of the best situation. You don't want to embarrass them into having to decline your offer or have them join you when they'd rather be somewhere else (nothing personal). Here's what you can say:

I'd like to celebrate by treating you to lunch or dinner. But, if you're strapped for time, let's just get a drink.

Would you like to join me for a celebratory bite to eat? Just let me know what time works for you.

As a special thanks, I'd love to tip a glass with you. What day works for you?

Please let me know if you can have a quick lunch or dinner. If you're busy—no worries. I'll take a rain check!

Do not ask for more leads should your contact accept. That's tacky. Give him a night to bask in your success and eat and drink up. Then, wait a few months or so depending on the person and your relationship. Then, shoot off an e-mail saying something like this:

Hope you're well. I'm still busy at the Hotchkins Group, although we've settled into a good (and relatively not stressful) relationship. I was hoping you and I could touch base again. What does your week look like?

My talk at the ASB Award ceremony went really well: I even got three new clients from it. Do you happen to know any other associations who would appreciate a talk on this subject matter? I'd love to hear about them.

I found your previous contact so helpful I was selfishly hoping you could pass along some more.

As always, reciprocity is key. If you and the contact have a good personal relationship, then invite her out socially. Otherwise, she may feel that you're using her:

Either way, want to get together for a drink?

I'd love to see you if you come to town. I won't be heading your way until December.

Are you free for lunch? We can catch up about everything else, too!

If she isn't interested, give her an out and thank her again:

If not, please know how much I appreciate your previous contacts.

As always, I appreciate all your efforts on my behalf.

If I can return the favor—or help you in the future—please let me know. I'd be happy to do so.

When the Previous Leads Didn't Work Out

The trick here is to not mention that the previous leads didn't work out, but that you appreciated your contact's help. You may add something specific—that the leads gave you helpful information or pointed you in a different direction. Here are some ideas:

Your last suggestions were really helpful—everyone gave me great insights. Since then, I've shifted direction somewhat and was hoping you could give me feedback.

I appreciate your previous suggestions—they helped me generate new approaches. Do you think we could talk again?

Since we last spoke in the fall, I've followed up on all your ideas and leads! Now I'm wondering if you'd mind giving me feedback.

When You Were in Touch with the Contact Recently

When contacting someone you spoke to recently, say something about your previous connection. Make it personal—the best possible contact is one who approaches you from an individual perspective:

Hope the snow cleared up and you were able to reach the office! We're dry as a bone here!

Hope things calmed down a bit and you can breathe a little easier.

Just checking in to see if you hired those new employees. If so, and you have time now, would you like to go out for a cup of coffee?

When we spoke last month, you mentioned that you were in the middle of completing an important proposal. Did you finish it on time? And even more to the point—do you think you'll be a winner?

Congratulations—I heard you're a grandmother now! Last time we talked, you were waiting!

Then, ask for whatever you need. Be conscious of the fact that you spoke recently:

I don't want to take up too much of your time, but I was hoping we could reconnect.

I had a few follow-up questions I'd like to ask you. Do you have any time this week?

Would you like to meet at the café again in the next week or two? I was hoping to ask a few questions.

If possible, offer something in return. If nothing comes to mind, think hard. Did your contact mention a book he or she liked? An author? Perhaps unusual and hard-to-find food? See if you can find it for him. Don't get anything elaborate: that will only embarrass him. Even better, see if you can offer something professional in return. Here are some ideas; the specifics will depend on your situation:

I'd like to give you a beautiful collection of Mark Twain's stories that I found in an antique store. I immediately thought of you when I saw it.

By the way, I found a can of those dried yellow peas you told me about—in New York City of all places. Anyway, I'll give them to you when we meet.

I just received copies of my new book. I'd like to give you a copy as thanks.

If you're up for it, I'd be happy to review your existing systems and make recommendations that could help you cut costs.

If you like, please bring a list of questions that you'd like me to address about the new developments. I might be able to help.

I can give you an interesting list of sales figures that I compiled— some of it from online sources and others from hard copy.

When You Haven't Been in Touch with the Contact

Think of this as striking up an old friendship. Remember: you want your contact to be open to you, so make sure you elicit excitement. Avoid sounding guilty or otherwise remorseful:

Do not:
I'm so sorry I haven't been in touch.

Boy, do I feel awful. I know I said I'd be back in touch in a few weeks and a whole year's gone by!

Sorry about the delay in getting back in touch with you.

I'm sorry I've taken so long to say hello. I'm so bad about keeping in touch, and I always regret it later!

And be positive and happy about the connection:

Although it's been a year since we were in touch last, I have been thinking of you often. How is your arm? I bet the break has healed by now. I also wanted to update you about my progress—I'm doing pretty well with help from your contacts.

Wow, has it really been a whole year since we've been in touch? We have to get together soon!

Where have you been? I figured I'd see you around at some point. I really wanted to update you about those contacts you sent me way back when . . .

I met you at your office last fall and you gave me some helpful information about the fishing supply industry. Since that time . . .

Even better, let her know if you've spent time and energy trying to find her:

I hope this e-mail reaches you safely! I tried contacting you at Edlesons, but the message bounced back. When I called, they said you moved on. So, after about half a dozen calls—here I am!

I've been trying to reach you for several months to see how you are and to update you since our last conversation. I finally ran into Jonny Weaver who said you were working at Stein's.

In all cases, be sure to ask about your contacts' lives as well as update them about yours.

When should you come out and directly ask them for leads without a formal phone call or a face-to-face meeting? That would depend on your relationship with the contacts. I have a good friend, Ellen Tunstall, who has sent me more contacts—and more work—than a girl could have hoped for. We've had drinks, dinners, and parties together. Yet, I met her in a professional setting and spent most of our relationship as a consultant working for her. If I need an idea, a lead, or information, I always ask. Usually, she gives me the answer I'm hoping for—then we meet for lunch anyway.

When a Project or Job Has Ended and You Need New Leads

How you approach this kind of communication depends on many factors: why you're moving on, your relationship with the contacts, how much they know about your previous assignment. Generally speaking, though, try to sound upbeat. This will encourage them to open up and feel good about you. Notice the difference:

Bummer words:
Unfortunately

Tough shape

Miserable

Unfair treatment

Sorry to say

Sadly

Horrible

Abusive (resist!)

Liars

Terrible

Bad experience

Fired

Fired

Fired [I know, I said this three times, but I mean it. The best of employees and contractors have been fired, but the word still has a stigma, much like, say, prisoner. It will be a red flag in any exchange—so don't do it!]

Better words:
Left

Moved on

Moving forward

Completed

Looking forward to

Heading in a new direction

Up ahead [as opposed to left behind]

Excited about the possibilities

Ready to go on to new challenges and places

If you left over a public scandal, whether or not it involved you directly—for instance, if a problem at the senior level closed down operations—be sure to take the contact into your confidence. Be honest without complaining:

I'm sure you heard what happened over at FFT & Sons last month. As you can imagine, we were as surprised as anyone else.

After 20 years at The Price Hunter I'm heading out into the world—I'm sure you know why!

Can you believe it: after a long successful life, we're finally closing shop. I'm sure you read about it in the newspaper, but things are even stranger than they seem!

When you were f . . . OK, let's just say "let go":

I've left.

I'm moving on after working at . . .

My project at Swanson has ended and I'm looking forward to new and equally exciting projects.

My company has completed our project at . . .

After consulting at LifeLine Insurance for the past five years, I'm moving on.

When other circumstances have caught up with you and your previous situation:

As you know, the economy has hit the newspaper business really hard. So, I'm moving into the world, hoping to find equally exciting and fulfilling opportunities in other forms of media.

As you probably know, the drought has caused many plants to close down, some indefinitely. So, I've found myself looking for a new career in the food industry and hoped you could provide some insights.

I, like so many others in the airline industry, are moving on to new areas of travel and tourism. And I thought who better to contact for great insights and ideas than you!

Part 2

Networking in Groups

Networking in groups, whether at a convention, conference, training session or, depending on how hard you push, a cruise, wedding, or other social occasion, is unlike any other interactive experience.

Let's start with the professional gathering. There you are surrounded by lots of other people, probably in your industry, who, in most cases, are also networking. All of you want something from each other besides the pleasure of simply interacting. You want leads. Insights. And the all-important handshake, should a deal transpire. Yet everyone there is pretending to be, well, purely social. Then there's that undercurrent of reciprocity. You offer them something and they offer you something back and vice versa. And, before you know it, you have a stack of business cards and lots of promises. Fun, interesting, and exhausting.

Your mission, should you choose to accept it, is to get as many of the right contacts as possible and only respond to those who can really help. If you *don't* choose to accept it, you'll be left with a whole lot of work. You'll get in touch with some good contacts, yes, but also plenty who have nothing real to offer but want to take, take, take from you.

Finally, there's the literal social networking opportunity. Watch out for this one. It can be tacky to peddle your wares, so to speak, at an event like a wedding. The bride and groom kissing, the parents crying with joy, and the band playing every wedding song available. And you, looking to garner leads for your business or job search? Eh—don't think so.

In these social situations, let the contacts come to you. You're sitting at the table and Uncle Mel (on the groom's side) asks what you do. You sell women's clothing to retail stores, you say. And Uncle Mel? You won't believe it! He's in the garment business. What do you know? Then he leans over between sips of scotch and slides his business card your way. He can help. You accept—and why shouldn't you? But a situation like that should be the only one where socializing and business meet. Anything short of that level of ease would be tacky.

As for the perfect phrases for networking at professional events? Oh, so many to choose from—and you'll find them in this section!

Chapter 7

The Big Venue: Conferences, Conventions, and Training Centers

Conferences, conventions, and training programs are, for all anyone cares to admit, educational events. But face it: everyone there is networking. People want jobs. They want customers. They want employees. And this means they want to network. So, approach these events as opportunities and make sure you stay open-minded about all that they offer.

Chance Meetings in the Halls

These meet-ups can be easy or awkward depending on your personality and theirs. Your best bet is to test the water by opening with chit-chat—a simple line or two—and seeing how the contact responds. A low-level sigh followed by a monosyllabic word or a grunt? Don't even bother. An open response, a joke, maybe, and you'll be set.

Your comment can be:

This is an amazing hotel, isn't it?

What did you think of the keynote speaker?

The weather's crazy out there, isn't it? I hope the airport is open tomorrow.

Did I see you reading The Ninth Estate *in the lobby earlier? It's my favorite book.*

. . . or just about anything else. Be sincere, by the way—not goofy. By which I mean using canned lines like "Didn't I meet you before," or "You look familiar," when they don't—and you didn't.

At a Luncheon or Dinner

Obviously, you'll introduce yourself and shake hands. Just be sure to mention something about your field of expertise, and show interest in theirs.

Use phrases such as:

John Jacobs, professor of environmental sciences at MIT.

Nice to meet you. I'm Deb Shaw—I own Deb's Soaps and Baths. How about you?

I'm Laura Bonet, of the Family Clinic. And you are . . . ?

Loren Scott of NBC Television, nice to meet you. And you are . . . ?

Then try to draw a natural connection between you:

Oh, you're at NBC Television? I used to work at NBC Radio in New York.

The Control Center has an amazing reputation for its innovative approaches. What's it like to work there?

Are you based in San Francisco? I lived there for almost fifteen years.

That's an interesting field. Where did you study?

Are you familiar with the work of Frank Wilson? He's written some amazing books—they're classics.

How do you like working for Norm Rogers? He has quite a reputation.

Don't say anything negative about their workplace or professional relationships, no matter how renowned:

Not these:
How are you guys handling the scandals?

Is Herb Havenwood as nasty a person as they say?

Do you really think your line of work is unethical? I know you get lots of bad PR indicating it is.

Are you comfortable working for a company with such a bad reputation?

Of course, you don't want to lie or feign ignorance, either. So, if the contact's company or other professional affiliation has been getting bad press, it's OK to check in, in the least judgmental way possible.
Stay upbeat:

How are things going at the company?

You think things will turn around soon?

How's the morale over there? Good?

You guys have been getting lots of publicity. How is it going?

Unless the conversation naturally flows in that direction, don't ask for leads right away. Instead, see if the contact is interested in getting together:

> *Do you want to get together after the conference ends tomorrow? The shuttle doesn't leave for a few hours.*
>
> *Maybe we could connect after the conference.*
>
> *Would you like to meet up later this week?*

Or just hand over your card and invite her to contact you. Be sure there's something in it for her:

> *Give me a call if you want. I can tell you some good sights to see when you visit Boston.*
>
> *Let me know when you come to St. Louis. I can introduce you to George.*
>
> *If you're interested in doing business with the envelope manufacturers, just let me know. My brother has been in the business forever, and I'll be happy to introduce you.*

You don't have to specify what's in it for you necessarily. They'll know.

Making Contacts in Training Sessions

At training sessions, it's really important that you respect the trainer and your fellow participants. So, don't network during the actual session—wait until later. But you can let attendees know a little bit about you by briefly (and I mean *briefly*) saying what you do in the context of the broader discussion.

Keep it short and relevant:

I have a question about how you'd apply that concept to my work at Cisco. We have a staff of 2,500, which is much greater than what you mentioned.

Or you could have said:

I have a question about how you'd handle larger groups of 2,500 or so staff members.

As a professor of urban studies at Vanderbilt, I'm curious about how your ideas apply to inner-city teens between fifteen and eighteen years old.

Or you could have said:

I'm curious about how your ideas apply to inner-city youth between fifteen and eighteen years old.

Here are a few more:

In my research for my book Age and Aging: An Adult Child's Guide, *I found that the statistics weren't that drastic. Can you provide more detail about what your findings involve?*

I wrote an article in that same journal and was surprised at the controversy it generated.

My company, Mercury, Inc., is small but aggressive. Do you have any insights for us?

Be on the alert! Listen to what your fellow participants have to say. If they introduce themselves at the beginning of the session, jot down names and professions or company names. You may want to network with them later.

If you do network later, make an immediate and personal connection:

> *I was really interested in what you said about the role of Jungian psychology in advertising.*

> *I heard you mention that you went to Princeton. So did my brother. It's an amazing school.*

> *I thought what you said in the seminar was really astute.*

Then, hand the contact a card or let the conversation roll. The more you talk and find commonalities, the more likely he will remember you when you contact him later.

Connecting with a Presenter

As I mentioned at the beginning of this chapter, most people at professional events are more than happy to network. Even in unofficial networking events, most people attend primarily to shake hands, collect cards, and garner leads and information later. That idea holds true for the presenter as well. In fact, many presenters see the payback for their training as getting contacts and winning work. So, you shouldn't hesitate to network with them. They see you as a contact, you see them as a contact, and all is well.

Naturally, say something about their session, such as how much you liked it:

> *I really enjoyed your presentation.*

> *You are an excellent presenter. Your sense of humor really helped motivate us!*

> *Great presentation.*

Or revisit a point that they raised:

I thought your approach to linking the two models was really amazing.

I had a few questions about the Feldership method. Do you have a minute?

Could you explain what you meant about the digestive processes of guinea pigs?

Where possible, offer your contacts something, such as an introduction to someone who will be helpful to them—and the other person. Remember: be authentic. Don't introduce people unless both will benefit.

Make your offer inviting:

I'd like to talk to my boss about your approaches. He may want to bring you in as a consultant.

Do you know Madeline Robinson? She wrote the book **Intelligent Today.** *I thought you might be interested in connecting with her.*

Our training department could really use someone like you. Shall I try to connect you?

Be sure to get their contact information. Be clear that you want to speak for your own purposes, too.

I'd like to ask you a few questions when I get in touch. Is that OK?

Could I contact you in the next few weeks? What do you prefer, an e-mail or a phone call?

I'm really interested in this field of study. Could I give you a shout in a few weeks for a short phone call?

I was hoping to join your company—in the IT area. Can I call you next week for some insights about the best approach?

If you proposed a connection at the event, make sure that you follow up with it when you contact them.

Is this bribery? Luring them in? Holding your contacts hostage until they give you the leads you require? Not at all. It's basic reciprocity also known as "You scratch my back and I'll scratch yours." But, if you feel funny about that aspect of the interaction, you have a few choices. Give them the connections you promised first, then wait a bit to follow up on your own behalf. Or, follow up with them without mentioning the leads. Then provide them later. As always: integrity first.

Connecting with Visitors at Your Booth

If you've worked the booth at conferences then you know that after the first hundred or so visitors, your eyes start to glaze over and you can hardly speak. Brain death? Exhaustion? Possibly both. So, be sure to take breaks, eat well, sleep well, drink plenty of water—and use the following perfect phrases.

Gather information by looking at visitors' badges so you can have a meaningful, initial interaction:

Oh, you work for the ASPCA. You do great things for the animal community.

Are you from PETA? My sister-in-law is a vegetarian.

I see you're from the Humane Society. Are you in the corporate office?

Are you from the New York or San Francisco office?

If they don't have a badge or other revealing information, then ask a pertinent question:

What company are you from?

Then follow up with questions to get the right kind of qualifying information:

What do you produce?

How large is your company?

What sector do you serve?

How long have you been around?

What kind do you produce?

How often do you ship?

Are you local or international?

Be sure that you express some interest—you don't have to get delirious, of course, but people are more willing to connect when they feel what they're saying is interesting and that they'll be appreciated.

That's interesting.

I never knew that.

Seriously? Who knew?

Thanks for telling me.

How long have you been doing that—I never heard about it!

Be honest with them—and yourself. For networking to truly work, your interest must be sincere. If you're getting bored or find the people annoying, take a break. If necessary, take a long break. First impressions really do last and last and last. If you feign interest and they know it (which they always do), you may never be able to backtrack.

Then, offer them a giveaway, contest ticket, coupon, or whatever gift you have at your booth to seal the deal:

Why not sign up for our lottery? You can win some pretty cool prizes.

Don't forget to take a chocolate. They're really good. Imported from Switzerland.

Would you like to sign up for our newsletter? We have coupons and giveaways.

If you're interested, we can send you one month for free.

Make follow-up plans, and keep it simple.

We'll be in touch with you.

We'll send you a newsletter.

Nice talking to you. I look forward to contacting you again.

Be sure not to make plans you can't keep. Otherwise, you'll seem unreliable. And, if they say they'll be in touch with you, give them a good reason to do so. Make it pressing. Like the tickets will expire, or you're looking into other companies and need to make a choice soon.

Doubtless, they will hand you a card. So, on the back, remember to write their level of interest and why you should get in touch. If you like, create a code for yourself so you can quickly keep track without having to take away valuable time from new visitors. For example, one star could mean high interest, two stars moderate interest, and three stars low-level interest, or the other way around. If someone strikes you as low level, by the way, don't give up. Send them a follow-up message through your mass distribution.

As for the high-level interest people, get in touch with them personally. This means that you should also dash down a few words such as where they come from, what they said about their company, and anything else that's helpful. Then, use these tidbits to establish your all-important opening line.

When following up with a visitor personally, be specific. The connection doesn't necessarily have to be about business:

> *We spoke at the conference about your cat Pretty Kitty. Are her hairballs under control?*

> *When we met at the conference, you mentioned that you were moving to a new office. Are you there yet?*

> *I really enjoyed talking to you about Dr. Howard. I think you are the only one there who ever heard of him—much less knew him.*

> *When we met at my booth, you mentioned that Mrs. Taylor's Cookies were the best. Well, I had the chance to try them!*

But if you had a business-only discussion or your contact would consider your comments chatter, not a personal connection, stay with professional matters:

> *You mentioned that you were interested in seeing the 2009 report, so I'm sending you a copy.*

> *We had an interesting discussion about the properties of the yucca root. I thought I'd give you some particulars that I found.*

> *We discussed the value of gold since the recent recession. I have some interesting information about that.*

When following up with a lower level contact, send a generic note as you can't spend the time writing endless personal connections:

Thanks so much for talking to us at the conference. I hope you enjoyed the chocolate.

Hope you enjoyed the conference as much as we did.

This year's conference was great: more people attended than ever before, and we were happy to be a part of it.

Then offer something your contacts can't resist:

In honor of the conference, we're giving away free boxes of our cookies.

We'll be happy to give you a free appraisal.

We're offering a 20 percent discount for a whole year to everyone who attended the conference.

Making Meaningful Connections at Other People's Booths

Finding the right contacts at other people's booths can entail some sneaky activities. For example, as you look at the brochures and papers at the booth, keep your ears open. If you hear information in the discussion that indicates someone is your perfect networking candidate, wait until the conversation is through. Then introduce yourself and draw an immediate connection:

I overheard you saying that you are in the robotics field.

I notice that your badge says you're from Sanitation, Inc.

Did I hear you say that you've been working in textiles since the 1980s?

I didn't mean to eavesdrop, but I thought I heard you say you were the leading manufacturer of widgets.

If you're planning to talk with another participant, let her finish the discussion with whoever is running the booth. This is common courtesy. If you want to lure away a contact so she gravitates to your company instead, do so after the contact has walked away from the booth. Remember: tackiness never works.

If you're approaching people who are running the booth, feel free to open in whatever way you like. After all, they're being paid to talk to you:

What does your company manufacture?

Do you develop tourism in East Africa as well?

I really like your display. It's amazing.

What do you guys do?

If you find a connection, jump on it:

I worked for TecCo years ago. They were one of the first to manufacture those!

Do you know Jane Pauley? She works there as well.

I read an article about your firm in Yesterday *magazine. Did you see it?*

Then get more information, get their card, and jot down your action plan on the back—after you've turned a corner where they can't see!

Chapter 8

Networking at the Networking Event

Talk about hunger. Nowhere in the networking world will you find more hunger than in the networking sessions themselves. There, everyone wants something from everyone else. Contacts. Suggestions. Inside scoops. Not to mention work, jobs, employees, sales, and all that (hopefully) follows. Some people are somewhat hungry. Others are starving. So remember: whether you're eagerly (or nervously) hunting down a job, eager to hurry up and find employees, or anxious to get sales leads, relax. Stay cool. Be centered. Because people are much more willing to pass on good information and seek you out if you come off as cool, calm, and together.

Creating the Perfect Three-Minute Description of Your Business

The three-minute "who I am" talks, a must at all networking meetings, can be maddeningly general, unless you prepare. So, before you go to the event, sit down and develop your talk, rehearse, and memorize it. Three minutes seem too short? No worries: that's about all the time you have to hold their attention anyway—after that, you really need to push.

Start by determining the most valuable attribute of your business or professional experience. You want to draft a list of the five or ten most positive aspects of the business and then narrow the list to the most impressive one. Yes, one. You only have three minutes, remember? By the way, be sure to take this from their perspective—not yours. This will make a remarkable difference in terms of how people respond to your presentation.

Do not focus on you:

My business is really creative and insightful. It's fair to say that practically everyone who works there has fun!

Even though the business is exhausting—and I don't get to see my kids half the time—I really like it.

We made a huge profit last year, in spite of the recession.

We've been in the industry for twenty-five years. The original founders still own it.

See, who cares? Why should they connect with you? Be interested in you? Even if those aspects of the business are relevant (people generally like to do business with family-owned and -operated enterprises), is this feature really the most important? Remember: you only have *three* minutes! Don't use a single extra word.

Do focus on what interests them:

We sell the highest-rated widgets in the northern hemisphere.

We specialize in creating advertising and marketing campaigns for the dental industry.

We are the largest brokerage firm in the Panhandle, serving more than three thousand new clients a month.

*We are experiencing rapid growth and are looking for new
employees to grow with us.*

Then, develop this one point by providing interesting (and captivating) support information. Remember that list you drafted earlier?
You may be able to add some of those points:

Our widgets have been featured on **60 Minutes** *and in the*
New York Times *Business section.*

*Our advertisements have won our clients 10–20 percent more
customers within the first year—more than any other form of
marketing.*

We continue to expand as our clients like and trust us.

*Our exit polls show that 95 percent of our employees value
their time with us and most would like to work for us again.*

*We have received the industry Customer Service Award three
years in a row.*

*The Safety Standards Board has given us commendations six
times since 2000.*

*We offer flexible hours, training opportunities, and amazing
benefits. [Right for employee hunters.]*

Never add too many support points—or too few. As in so many things,
three tends to be a good number. Be sure to have some order to your
points: perhaps make one more exciting than the next; have all your
support points be of equal import, then close with a bang; focus on
one amazing support point in great detail; and so on. Think this sounds
like marketing? Guess what? It is!

And remember: at most networking events, person after person
will be clamoring for attention whether from a high-profile individual
or from everyone else. Your talk must compete!

Creating the Perfect Three-Minute Description of Your Qualifications

If you thought the three-minute description of your business was hard, the three-minute description of yourself—whether you're a contractor, self-employed artisan, or professional searching for a job—is even harder. Here's why: in our society, you simply can't talk about your strong points without people thinking that you're bragging. Besides, you don't have credibility with this particular audience. You're at a networking event, right? You're talking about yourself? What are you supposed to say? You're a failure? An overall annoying guy? A dud? Of course not!

So, what do you do? Follow the same rules that we've established for businesses—and remember these perfect points:

Don't brag:

I am a really successful attorney.

People really love me. How could they not?

Anyone who hires me will be glad she did.

I'm probably the smartest person in the business.

Do be objective and clear:

I've only lost one court case.

I was voted the head of my union at the company and given the Employee of the Year award.

I will bring the same energy and focus to my new position as I did to the past—which won my last employer 25 percent more profits within a few months.

Although I have a Ph.D., I consider true intelligence the flexibility to learn new skills.

If you must discuss how great you are, let other people do the talking. For example, get other people to proclaim your value or attribute the positive comments to someone else:

My editor said I was brilliant. And I did my best to prove him right.

They say they hired me because of my smarts.

On the evaluation, every reviewer noted my tenacity and hard work.

My clients have said that I provide friendly service, regardless of the situation.

My boss said she admired my patience. At times, I even surprised myself.

Still, show what you've done in all cases and let listeners understand your value for themselves.

Creating the Perfect Ten-Second Elevator Speech

If the three-minute spiel was a press release, this is an ad. In fact, many ads really are ten seconds or less—and it takes even less time for an audience to judge the value of a website, song, or marketing piece. So, cheer up: ten seconds isn't so short after all. Here's what you do:

Use strong verbs—they give energy to the short talk:

Weak:
I got the President's Award.

My company has a stellar reputation in research.

Our sales rate went up.

Strong:

I was honored with the President's Award.

My company can boast a stellar reputation in research.

Our sales rate skyrocketed.

Use metaphors:

We approach every situation with the power of a jet engine.

We have the integrity of a Boy Scout in a field that's bearish.

The green grass of our industry can have many splinters—but we're prepared.

Pose a question:

If you could save money on your electric bills—and get twenty-four-hour service—why wouldn't you?

Of course people use our service. We've been voted number one for ten years in a row. Why wouldn't they?

Do you know that I won the gold medal in Olympic swimming in 1985? And I bring that same energy and determination to my sales position.

You may wonder what the best approach could be. We wrote a book about it—and it's been translated into twenty-eight languages.

Make sure your ten-second spiel has some element they'll remember for good—and may even encourage contacts to find you later.

Make a promise. An amazing point. Something to make them laugh. Even a challenge:

> *I challenge anyone to send along a car problem that I can't solve.*

> *I challenge you to answer these questions. If you get them right, I'll give you three hours of consulting for free.*

> *Here's a challenge: figure out the formula we used and I'll show you how to apply it.*

Be creative. Have fun. And your contacts will be networking about you before long!

Determining if the Contact Is Worthwhile

You really do need to qualify your leads much as a salesperson does. Otherwise, you might be wasting your time on people who won't get you far—or anywhere, actually. But be discreet. Here are three of the most important qualifying attributes you should hunt for:

- They have longevity in the profession or company. This is important, so ask—it's easy:
  How long have you worked for the company?
  Have you been doing this long?
  How many years have you been in practice?
  When did you start your practice?

- They like where they work. Negativity can mean doors close behind them. And if they do, you probably don't want these folks to escort you in!
  How do you like the job?

Do you enjoy speaking to other people all day?

What is it like to talk down people who are really depressed?

Are you happy in your field?

Do you plan to stay in this field for a long time?

What is the best thing about where you work?

- They're willing to get you in touch with other people. Otherwise, they may have left bad blood behind them:

Do you know anyone who can help me navigate the application process?

Who's a good person to talk to?

Do you know anyone who can answer these questions?

I'm curious about the procurement department—I'd like to become a supplier. Do you know anyone I can talk to there?

Setting Expectations

In any networking situation, your role is to give as well as take. By give, of course, I mean give those all-important leads. But how many leads can you provide? And how soon can you get them out? Who can you call back or e-mail immediately? Who will have to wait? OK, you may be wondering why these questions are important. Etiquette, you think. But there's another reason.

If you set people's expectations high and then let them down, they'll think negatively of you. And when you need the leads from them, they may be unwilling. Besides, your networking universe will grow tighter and tighter the longer you're in it. So, you want to have a great reputation on all fronts and in the eyes of as many people as possible. Here are some perfect phrases for setting expectations when you don't want to disappoint.

When you are promising a time to get back in touch:
I'll be traveling quite a bit this month but will be in touch when things calm down.

I have two enormous reports that are due by the end of the quarter. Why not get in touch then?

I'll probably follow up after the summer vacation; too many employees are out, and I'll need to fill in.

Want to talk in early September, once things start hopping again?

Be honest about these reasons. Why aren't you getting in touch right away? What other priorities are ahead of this connection? Then mention them. You're not trying to lie or manipulate but be honest. If the person is a low priority, let the timing be vague and the venues relatively easy for you to manage.

When the person is a low priority:
I come to Maine every few months. I can get in touch with you on my next trip—maybe we'll have lunch?

Why not e-mail and stay in touch. If something interesting crops up, I'll be sure to let you know.

I'll add you to my newsletter list: I keep a log of events that will probably interest you.

When promising to send along contact information:
I'll be out of the office quite a bit and will need to look up a few things before I get in touch.

I'll contact the office manager about an informational phone call. But remember: she's really busy and who knows when I'll hear back.

Why don't you e-mail me, and I'll let you know my progress.

I may forward your information to Connie Stevens. She may be able to help you.

Be sure that if you promise to follow up, you do. It's rude not to. If you can't reach the person, as promised, or don't have the time to give the information you promised, let your contact know.

What to say when you can't keep a promise:
I tried reaching Connie, but she isn't returning my messages. If I do hear back, I'll let you know.

The names that I promised seem to be evasive—I can't find some and can't reach the others for approval. Should anything yield, or if I have better ideas, I'll let you know.

Sorry to take so long getting back to you. It seems that the VP left her position, and I know very little about her replacement.

Sorry, I can't connect you to the team as promised. I did hear that two others may be good, though: Honeywell and Junipers. Good luck in contacting them—I hope it works out.

As always, be sure that you're sincere. Lies sound hollow and, besides, why bother? The truth is just as good, since the outcome is the same for your contact.

Getting the Names of Decision Makers

The first step in getting the name of a decision maker is to have a strong connection with the contact. That person must like and trust you; otherwise, why would he or she give out contact information about the senior-most levels of the organization? If you don't have that connection, you can still ask. But chances are you may only get the most general response—information you can easily get online.

Here are some perfect phrases; they're direct and intuitive:

Do you know anyone in the CEO's office?

I'm looking for someone like John Henry—remember him?

Is Manny Horowitz still in the HR department?

Who should I talk to in Accounting?

Who's the new VP? Is she easy to talk to?

Is your CMO open to meeting consultants?

Chapter 9

Networking When You're the Star

I just have to tell you about this networking faux pas because it's so classically bad. Years ago, when I was a college professor, I had to attend a weeklong professional development program. One of the speakers was a psychologist giving a presentation on anxiety and stress.

I don't remember if the subject matter was our anxiety, the students' anxiety, or—who knows?—his own, but he began by saying: "Before I get started, I'm going to do the usual: you know, pass out my card and tell you about my services." Huh? We were there to learn new skills. Get insights into a new subject matter. We were most certainly *not* there as networking targets for him.

The moral of the story: even though you're the star, discretion is everything.

A few other pointers before we delve into perfect phrases: First, in every group, only a few participants will have the names or information you're after. Many may be mildly interested, while others may have no interest at all. They attended your session because it was interesting to them in a small way but not something they want to pursue. If you make the mistake of speaking to those people only, you'll have plenty of unhappy people in your audience.

Second, the adage "Show, don't tell" works well here. Throughout your talk, show them how you've brought success to clients or others like them. Don't use names and don't focus on yourself. Talk about them. Their experience. And their successes. Don't overdo it—use personal experience now and then. This will encourage the right people to approach *you* when you're done!

Third, put your contact information on everything: your cards, training materials, giveaways. And get their contact information, too. The universe of networking is expansive; you'll be hearing from people unexpectedly. And, of course, the more often you keep in touch, the more likely they'll network with you.

Discreet Networking During a Talk

So how do you talk about yourself, reveal your great ideas, and underscore your value without actually saying it? Talks are *the* perfect venue. Just mention a client (not necessarily by name) or the results you were able to get as an example to support your point. This works well for everyone: you get to talk about yourself and the listener gets value by hearing an example. Obviously, the perfect phrases will depend on your experience and the content of your talk. But here are some generic examples that can help give you ideas.

Use your experience and accomplishments as an example:

One example of how a business resolved this issue occurred with one of my clients . . .

The best example I can think of happened to a client of mine way back in the 1990s when . . .

A really funny example of this is . . .

I had a client who had an interesting experience with this . . .

One of my clients needed to . . .

One of the worst experiences I can remember occurred with a client who _____. They resolved it by . . .

For example, one client . . .

Years ago, I was called in to . . .

One manufacturing company was in a transition period much like what you're experiencing now. So, here's how we solved its problem . . .

Show that their problem, which seems huge and insurmountable to them, is routine from your perspective:

I've seen this kind of situation countless times.

You can manage this problem quite quickly—and inexpensively—in many ways. Here are a few examples.

I've seen companies solve this problem in a number of ways. The most common is . . .

One of the best ways to create a better . . .

Most executives feel almost paralyzed by these dilemmas. It's helpful to know that they have occurred since the beginning of business and will occur again. Let me tell you a few success stories that I've experienced.

Here are a few case studies from my work over the years.

The examples are too numerous to count. Here are two that have impressed me the most.

In a Q&A session, let questioners know why their specific situation requires a specific solution and that you can help them find it:

I can't say for sure—I'd need to know specifics about your situation—but here are some ideas.

As you know, every situation is different and requires a specific solution. Here is what I can tell you, though.

The best way to figure it out is to look at your company history and see what you can find.

That really depends on a number of factors particular to your company. Some recommendations are . . .

Send them to your website, book, or information package. Make sure your contact information is plastered everywhere!

Make sure they find information they can use right away and not just promotional material for your business:

If you want more information, go to my website. I have lots of pointers.

If you look at my information packet, you'll find plenty of ideas.

Our website has a whole section of case studies that you'll find interesting.

I actually devoted a whole chapter to that very subject in my newest book.

If you want more information, check out my blog. I put in lots of links so that you could find more expert advice.

Do not bring up fees or other financial matters. If someone asks how much you charge, say you'll discuss after the session or recommend that the person leave his card. Do not treat your talk as an opportunity to sell your service: just let the audience know what you do in a way that's relevant to the information you're providing.

Discreet Networking After a Talk

If your talk is really good, you'll be able to win the hearts (and minds) of your audience. Most likely, people will come up to you immediately after the talk or later, asking you questions and commenting on some of your points. This is where you can make a (subtle) networking pitch. Here's how:

Do not ask questions that are intentionally negative or put the person on the defensive.

Do not:

Your line of work sounds really tense. Is it as bad as it sounds?

Your boss seems like a control freak.

Wow, what a nightmare.

I can see how difficult that situation must be. It must keep you up at night.

I think your company is really dysfunctional.

The industry is archaic, let's face it.

I think the industry is in big trouble and better shape up.

Do ask questions that will create a familiar relationship, where you're the trusted confidant.

Do:

How long has this been going on?

Do you have a broad enough customer base?

What do you think the major factors were that led to this situation?

How have you resolved these issues in the past? What's different now?

What are your main concerns, in terms of moving forward?

Do you think these are based in fact?

How does your team feel about these matters?

Do you need to win executive support?

Identify holes in their information, where obvious:

What you'd need to know is how much of a loss you can handle. It may be more than you think.

Find out how many employees are still working before you make any decisions.

What is the company mission?

Do you know how close you've stayed to the business plan?

Be positive where you can. They'll associate you later with that good feeling:

I know there are countless possibilities.

The situation may be better than you think.

You can move ahead at a faster rate than you assumed.

There are definitely more solutions to the problem than are apparent.

Of course, their business or industry may be in great shape—and hoping to get better. Definitely point that out:

You're really doing well, especially given the economy.

So, it seems like you're doing a great job and are ready to move to the next step.

Good work. You sound like a bright bunch of people.

Your organization seems to be really advanced.

Offer to contact the decision maker or boss:

If you'd like, I can contact your boss.

Do you think I should contact her?

Who is the best one to contact?

I may be able to present the idea to . . .

Does your group hold brown-bag lunches or other gatherings where I could present these ideas? They may find them interesting.

What is the best way to reach someone in your company?

Do you think I should contact someone there?

See if you can use their name. A personal connection can be of infinite value:

Can I say you said to contact them?

May I use your name?

Should I say you sent me?

Would it be appropriate if I mentioned your name?

It's always best for your contacts to call on your behalf in advance. Don't be shy about asking—just make sure they have an out if they'd rather not.

Getting Leads from Other Presenters

With other presenters, the discussion can go one of two ways: the presenters can see you as competition or as a partner. Obviously, you want to partner as much as possible. The best way to do this is to find commonality.

Introduce how you complement each other or have areas of expertise that overlap slightly:

I noticed that you were giving a presentation about verbal communications. I was discussing written communications.

You're in the movie industry? So am I!

Are you an agent? What kind of books do you represent?

Or determine what you have in common:

Which conferences have you attended?

I'm interested in your experience at . . .

Have you ever experienced . . . ?

Do you ever go to . . . ?

Then see if you can find joint projects or networking opportunities you can share:

I probably have clients who would value your insights.

Since your work complements mine, I wonder if we could present together at some point.

Getting Leads from the Event Planners

There's no question that giving a presentation is the best networking opportunity in the universe. OK, there's one better: when you get paid to give the presentation and get leads when you do. Either way, the event planner will be your best friend. That person can bring you in, recommend you, and essentially network you into the networking web.

Let her know what you think of the conference, and be specific:

You had a really great turnout. It was wonderful to see.

The variety of vendors was amazing. I think the participants really learned a lot from them, too!

Everything was so well organized.

Say what you liked about the talk:

They were a lively bunch!

I really enjoyed giving the talk! They asked really smart questions.

They were really engaged in the discussion.

They raised some interesting points that led to lively discussions.

Do not let yourself be vulnerable, so avoid situations where you can sound insecure or give her a window for letting in negativity:

Do not:
I'm interested in finding ways I can improve my presentation.

Did you hear any feedback about my talk?

I hope people liked my presentation. I enjoyed giving it and worked hard to make it good. [Intentions don't count— outcome does!]

If you have any feedback, let me know.

I look forward to getting the evaluations. I'm always interested in new ways to improve my talk.

People seemed to like my talk. What do you think?

Once you've established a personal relationship, see what she's interested in presenting for future sessions:

What other kinds of topics do your members want to know about?

Are there any particular areas in this field that you'd like to see addressed?

What are the most popular sessions?

What do you think the participants most value about the sessions?

I know that people enjoy sessions on Emotional Intelligence. Do you think they'd like something on a new area called Visceral Understanding? It's fascinating.

Or, when possible, offer her something she won't be able to resist:

I have a new video coming out in June. If you'd like, I can send you a copy.

I have a new book coming out. If you'd like, I can give a talk on the content. It should generate even more publicity than my last book, and your members will be the first to hear about it.

We have a new predictability model we developed. We could give you an exclusive for your newsletter in time for the next conference.

Remember that networking is an ongoing affair. Every marketing piece you write, business card you develop, logo you design, and talk you give is a networking opportunity. So, be sure you place good contact information on each of these and in plenty more places:

- Website
- Brochures
- Business cards
- Newsletter
- Holiday greeting cards
- Proposals
- Invitations
- Ads
- Posters
- Calendars and other gift items
- Window displays
- Signs
- Press kits
- Packaging
- Bags and other containers

Part 3

Online Networking

Online networking has moved quickly from being a little-known concept to attracting millions and millions of people through virtual inroads. Networking online is more complex than most people think. Yes, you do need perfect phrases that attract the visitor and resonate right away. But you also need to spend a lot of time getting to know people, combing through comments and contacts, and positioning your information so it escalates on the search engines.

The perfect phrases here should help a lot—but you should also seek out as much information as possible about how to use all the amazing tools available to you. I already mentioned search engine optimization, where you get your website or blog to have center stage when someone searches for your topic. But look into the various networking possibilities from Twitter to MySpace—and don't forget YouTube. Who knows, it could help. Every additional platform is good.

Regardless of where you are in cyberspace, a single concept reigns in the online world: anything goes! Because that universe is shifting so dramatically, the rules are unformed. So, be creative. Experiment. And see what others are doing. The online networking universe offers amazing possibilities—grab the ones that are yours!

Chapter 10

E-Mails

A whole chapter devoted to e-mails? Well, yes. These babies seemed to sprout up at the end of the last century and become a staple of networkers, internal communications, marketers—well, everyone. Yet, there weren't a whole lot of rules about the best way to get someone's attention in an e-mail, and there still aren't. So this chapter will be critical to your networking success.

Here are some basics; you'll find the perfect phrases in a minute:

- **Have a compelling subject line.** In a few words you must get the contact's attention, show her why she should open your e-mail—and why she cares about the content. Therefore, you have to be exciting, cool, intriguing, but not even remotely spam-like. Also make sure the contact knows your identity. If she won't remember your name, remind her of your identity right there.

- **Limit your e-mail to one or two paragraphs.** Unless you're sending a newsletter, keep it short, as in one or two paragraphs. One unnecessary word and you've lost them. On the other hand, when done well it can be captivating.

- **Avoid attachments, if possible.** Make the e-mail easy. Attachments ask too much of a person who doesn't know you. Even if you have an e-newsletter, keep all the text right there in the e-mail, with links if they want to learn more. Chances are, they won't open the attachment and may even dismiss your e-mail altogether.

Subject Lines to People Who Know You

If you have an informal relationship, make sure your subject line is informal, too. That sets a friendly and open tone that encourages your contacts to look at your e-mail and respond appropriately:

Where have you been?

It's me—I'm back!

HEY!

Are you out there?

Long time, no see

Guess what . . .

Make sure that the subject line and the first line of the e-mail have a direct connection:

Believe it or not . . . [The first line of the e-mail can be: "It's me!"]

Thinking of you . . . [The first line of the e-mail can be: "It's been a year since we last talked!"]

So much to say . . . [The first line of the e-mail can be: "Thanks to you I have been leading an exciting life!"]

You'll never believe . . . [The first line of the e-mail can be: "Who I ran into today."]

Should you invite a contact/friend out for a drink or bite to eat, especially when you're hoping to get leads? The answer is "yes," as long as you truly like the person. You don't have to mention that you want the leads, by the way, or even ask for them. If you mention your aspirations, good contacts will volunteer their help.

Subject Lines to People Who Don't Know You

These are tricky: if they're not strong, the contact will never open your e-mail. Then again, the contact won't open them if you sound too sales-y, inappropriate, overly appropriate. In other words, you must somehow find the right balance in your e-mail to get the contact to trust you enough to click on your e-mail.

Usually you will want to either conjure the name of someone you have in common—always useful if you were referred:

Peggy Doyle said to contact you . . .

Steve Walsh referral

Recommended by Francis Farmer

Hello from Jane Franks

A friend of Patricia Salvatore

Hello—Matt sent me!

Or mention someone—or someplace—you may have in common:

My Grandfather—Fred Harris

Northeastern Graduate inquiring

Sorority Member '06

Fellow organizer here!

Met on campaign?

You can always show your contacts the benefits of your message as well:

Sales opportunity

May 14 event!

Are you interested in . . .

Hoping to talk . . .

Subject Lines When You Briefly Met Face-to-Face

Your name may not be enough to trigger their memory, so mention the place where you met as well:

Met you at the NFTI Conference

Cindy from JFK Airport!

Hello from San Fran.

Your fellow passenger from France flight

Talked at SBIT lunch

Remember me? Stan from Chicago

Or tell them about yourself, if it's interesting:

The Van Man!

Peter's Assistant here

Sheila—the Avon Lady

Jan, the CPA from Dallas

Or, maybe you promised some sort of follow-up: someone's name, numbers, addresses. You can even mention that in the subject line, especially if it's more compelling:

The numbers for ASPO

The information you wanted in D.C.

Sending you the survey answers

About those lists . . .

The correct information as discussed!

Subject Lines When You've Already E-Mailed Them

This one is definitely touchy. You e-mailed them, but did they e-mail you? You may be tempted to lie and say something like you wanted to be sure they received your message. Or, your message bounced back. But one way or another they'll know—either your message was too obvious or too unlikely—especially if they saw that "bounced" e-mail and didn't bother to respond. So, you need to be honest and clear— and just a wee bit pushy. When you e-mailed once before, you can use any of the subject lines from before, with openings like:

Reconnecting . . .

Still trying . . .

Sent e-mail . . .

Or use perfect phrases like these:

E-mail—did you receive?

Trying to reach you?

Connecting?

Or, you can simply resend the e-mail.

Send an "oh-no" e-mail. This only works for people who are known for having a good sense of humor or are informal in style:

Oh no—my e-mail?

Oops—junk mail struck?

Oh no! Did you get . . .

For the more suit-and-tie types, forget this approach.

Warning: Exclamation points and unusual punctuation can help give your subject lines a lift, but they may also cause them to be picked up as spam.

When a contact ignores you twice, you have to make a decision. If the contact isn't of true importance, let it go. You only have so much energy to expend on your networking efforts—why waste a moment of it? Or, as the saying goes: so many contacts, so little time.

If the person is a significant contact, you need to decide why she didn't respond to your e-mail. Was a gatekeeper in the way? Did your e-mail wind up in the junk box? Did she simply delete it? Then, troubleshoot. If there's a gatekeeper in the way, perhaps you should call and chat with that person—get a sense of the best way to reach your contact.

Your communication may look something like this:

I was trying to e-mail Ms. Steward, but she didn't respond. Can you recommend the best way to reach her?

I sent Ms. Steward an e-mail last week but didn't hear back. Is there a better way to reach her?

I was trying to reach Mr. Dolan. Do you know the best way to get through? By e-mail? Phone call?

Doubtless, the person will ask about the nature of your contact. So, tell him the truth—but leave out any indication of neediness:

Do not:
I'm looking for a job and thought he could help me.

I'm in sales and someone thought she'd be a good source.

I'm trying to network.

I need help trying to get new clients.

I'm trying to make inroads in the field and I thought, why not start at the top?

Do:
I was hoping to have an informational talk for just fifteen minutes.

My colleague, Will Taylor, is a friend of his family. He recommended that I talk to him for some advice.

As a fellow graduate of MIT, I was hoping to connect and discuss some opportunities. [If this is too much of a stretch, don't use it.]

Several people in CNT referred me to her as a valuable source for information. Do you know the best way I can ask a few questions?

If you do ask for help—don't worry. As we discussed before, people love to give help. This help should come in the way of information. You can also ask for names, although the person may be reluctant to provide any—he'll help you but he doesn't want to burden someone else without permission. Of course, if you state your case well, he may even offer. And he may recommend people without giving you the OK to use his name.

Once you've talked to the assistant, send your follow-up e-mail—see if the assistant can recommend a subject line so the e-mail moves forward. The options are limitless. Here are a few:

(Your name)'s new e-mail

Brief talk?

Fellow alumni request

Getting Them to Respond to Your E-Mail

We've spent all this time talking about perfect phrases for subject lines because these three or four words are the gatekeepers of your text. Next, though, you must contain a riveting, or at least compelling, text within your e-mail that gets the response you want.

Start by reinforcing the subject line:

If the subject line was: *Peggy Doyle said to contact you . . .*

Say: *Peggy Doyle, my neighbor, said to contact you.*

If the subject line was: *Hello from Jane Franks*

Say: *Our mutual colleague Jane Franks recommended that I contact you and sends her regards.*

If the subject line was: *Met you at the NFTI Conference*

Say: *Great meeting you at lunch at the NFTI Conference. That was the most unusual ham sandwich I ever ate!*

If the subject line was: *Sheila—the Avon Lady*

Say: *Hope you remember me; we met at the Beauticians Conference. I'm the one you guys called the "Avon Lady" (ha-ha) even though I work for Revlon.*

Then, state why you're contacting them and what you hope they'll provide:

Peggy thought you might be able to give me advice about my new career in insurance. I made the switch recently after working for a brokerage firm.

Jane recommended that I contact you for information about . . .

At lunch, we discussed the possibility of exchanging client lists.

We discussed getting together for a chat about the industry—I thought that would be great!

Add relevant detail, but not too much—e-mails should be brief. Then put in your request:

Do you think we could get together for fifteen minutes or so next week? I'd be happy to meet at your office.

Want to schedule a conference call with my associate and me? I know we could come up with some great ideas.

What are you doing the week of March 5? I'll be in town and was thinking we could "do lunch" again, as they say.

I'd like to talk with you by phone or in person. Let me know which works best for you.

Getting Them to Contact Someone on Your Behalf

Generally, don't take this step until you've spoken to the contact and let him know you are reliable and trustworthy. However, if your referral recommends that you put in a request, go ahead. Or, you can ask more generally. Be tactful!

Use phrases like these:

She thought you might be open to introducing me to your boss.

Would you mind sending me contact information about the HR executives? I can use your name or not, depending on your comfort level.

I'd like to contact Ron Benson. Would you be able to give me information about the best way of doing so?

Sheila thought you might introduce me to the association board of directors. I'd be happy to send along any information about my qualifications.

Getting Them to Follow Up on a Previous Request

I was hoping to contact Bob Jeremy. Did you have a chance to reach him?

If possible, could you connect with Scott, as we discussed last week. Then, I'll follow up.

I'd like to contact the board of directors before their annual meeting. Did you have a chance to reach Mason?

Don't want to be a nudge, but were you able to contact Frank about my calling him? I want to talk with him before I send the mailing.

Be appreciative:

Many thanks.

I appreciate your help, as always.

Once again, thank you.

Thank you, as always.

Chapter 11

Networking Through the Social Network

Online Social Etiquette

Social networks are interesting things. Some people love them and spend more time there than at actual gatherings. Others limit their interaction, get involved with trepidation, or avoid them altogether. So, how much you rely on formal social networks depends on who you're trying to reach and why. Frequently, the breakdown occurs along age lines: Generations Y and X, people who are roughly between school-age and, let's say, their forties, are more likely to have a Facebook page than baby boomers are. But the trend is heating up, and now people of all tastes and ages have entered the social cyber sphere.

Another significant factor: the network you choose to engage in. You can always join the monster-size networks like LinkedIn, Facebook, and MySpace, where you can meet loads of "friends" and network with old friends, too; but you risk getting lost in the crowd. Or you can join so-called niche networks that are specific to your field or area of interest, although these don't have the wide reach of the other networks. While smaller, they may give you just the connection you need. But be aware: every company, association, marketer, and, well, everyone else has a social network. And you have only so much time. So choose wisely.

How you act within these universes is another matter. Most social networks are less than ten years old—many less than five years old. This means that the rules haven't been cemented and, while *not* everything goes, plenty more is acceptable than you find in traditional media. Nonetheless, here are a few rules of social etiquette that will create true networking opportunities.

Put your best face forward. Make sure that your visitor sees the best aspects of who you are—without any bragging involved.

Definitely do not:
I am a foremost expert in . . .

I enjoy a stellar reputation as . . .

Amazingly, I am the best at . . .

People think I'm really great . . .

Not to brag, but . . .

I am the founder of the Internet . . .

Go ahead and do:
I have almost thirty years of experience in technology. In fact, I was one of the original employees at IBM.

I was lucky enough to win the All-Star Award three years in a row!

I developed several concepts that are now used in . . .

Of course, if you are starting out and as fresh as a two-day-old baby, go ahead and say it:

I'm just entering the field . . .

As a newbie in online publishing . . .

Just left my number-crunching life as a CPA to fulfill my ambitions of being an artist . . .

Then ask for the advice or other information you want. But be specific: to start a real "conversation" or get helpful comments, you need to narrow the scope.

Less brings on more:

Anyone know any galleries that are open to new painters? I'll travel, but the New York area is best for me.

I'm hoping to find some associations that will help me get information and job opportunities.

I'm finding this universe difficult to navigate. Can anyone tell me where to go for some really great tips?

I need to find employees for low money and high commission. It's a sweat investment that will definitely pay off!

The idea of a social network is that you're all "friends" and everyone should help everyone else, as much as humanly (and virtually) possible.

Avoid corporate-speak. Note the word *social* in social networking. That means you're communicating in a person-to-person, not in an industry/sales/professional-only sort of way. You're having what social-networking types call "conversations." If you're not sure of just how these conversations work, imagine the person is sitting in front of you. With a big bowl of pretzels. And a beer.

No, no, no:
Pursuant to the last comment . . .

It has been brought to my attention that . . .

I am requesting that . . .

Owing to the fact that . . .

As a result of the . . .

Do:
I agree with your comment, but . . .

Sam e-mailed me that . . .

Could any of you . . .

Would anyone know . . .

Because of the . . .

I just found out that . . .

The AP Newswire reports that . . .

Create a dialogue:

The possibilities are endless. But how do you tap into them?

How many associations are there? How can you tell the difference between them? And what can you expect to get from them?

Who knows what makes this industry tick?

Or, speak directly to your visitor:

So what is the next step? I'd like to find out.

Does anyone know a great place to go to make connections?

I'm curious about the best way to get good guests. Can anyone offer advice?

Has anyone had luck going through those channels?

You can name names as well. But be cautious about slandering a person or organization. It speaks poorly of you, will make others in your network not trust you, and could possibly reach the person or people you're talking about (things have a way of traveling on the Internet!).

Do not:
NBCD has got to be the most dysfunctional place on the planet.

Rumor has it you shouldn't trust Billy Wild if your career depended on it.

Watch out for the folks at KLMT.

Ellen Rothstein is a jerk.

Rumor has it Folklore Inc. is pretty sleazy. True?

Does anyone know whether Todd Rudgin is as dishonest as I've heard?

Do:
Can anyone tell me their experiences at NBCD?

I'm interested in reaching someone at Telemundo. I only know one person—Ellen Rothstein. Does anyone have other people to recommend?

I'm interested in Folklore Inc. Can anyone give me insights into their business model?

Creating a Message That Invites Leads

Depending on the social network, you may not feel comfortable asking for leads. Perhaps you're in a professional network and are among friends—as well as competitors. Or perhaps the environment or culture of your social community doesn't allow for that kind of interaction. In that case, you may need to get leads in a more indirect route.

Ask a provocative question:

Anyone know the best way to get word out about this product?

What are the best ways to find information about this?

Wouldn't it be great to reach 200, maybe 300 people without having to pay for a list? Anyone have ideas?*

Let your network know your mission:

I'm hoping to find a really great job in development. Money means less than a great future, although I do want to get paid!

I'm starting up a really cool technology service. Check it out at my website and tell your friends!

I'm trying to build a strong team of visionaries who will take my business to the next step!

Many networkers find that by merely mentioning their situation or goals, "friends" will leap right in offering everything imaginable to help—and then some.

Getting Online Friends to Have Links to Your Site

Perhaps one of the greatest all-time networking opportunities is to get people to link your site to theirs. This can drive people to your site and elevate your search engine standing. How do you ask people to link your site? Here are some ideas:

Ask away:
Would you be willing to put a link on your site?

I want people to know my site is up and running. Could you put a link on your site?

Could you put a link for my site on yours?

I want people to find the regular updates and fresh information on my site. Think you could put a link in yours?

Ask and offer:
I'd like to put a link to your site on mine. Would you be willing to return the favor?

Want to link each other's sites? We have the same types of visitors, and we'd both get lots of new interest.

Shall we link? [for contacts with a sense of humor]

I put a link to your site on my website. Let me know if you're willing to return the favor.

Creating Comments That Imply Your Ability to Give Advice

Feel free to position yourself as an expert whom others go to for advice, but be discreet, as always. Information you provide about yourself should occur naturally within the context of your comments. So, discuss your experience:

In terms of years:
After spending the past fifteen years in the field, I have found that the reality is quite different.

As a twenty-year veteran of this . . .

Owing to my decades-long experience as a . . .

My ten years as a CMO have proven that . . .

Although your point is good, I know from ten years in the field that . . .

In terms of key events:
I conducted a significant amount of research on this matter (my findings were published in Psychology Today*). So, I can say that quite clearly . . .*

I won the Peabody Award for my research in that area, and my findings quite clearly indicate that . . .

The reality, as I expressed in my study "The Mating Habits of Toads," actually proves that . . .

In terms of affiliations:
I was a member of the department at the time this occurred, and quite clearly . . .

As a research fellow at the University of Delaware . . .

As jazz critic for the Cincinnati Free Times *. . .*

Creating Comments That Inspire Other Comments

You don't want to be difficult or insulting, but you can engage others by making definite and compelling points. In the process, you may generate conversations, comments, and networks of your own.

Generate more comments through phrases like these:

If anyone knows an exception, I'd like to know about it.

I'd be interested in learning about additional research.

Where can you find those kinds of recordings? And why aren't they more readily available? That's the question we're all hoping to have answered.

This is an ethical issue—not simply a logistical one. [Phew! Who could resist commenting on that!]

Using a Blog as a Networking Tool

There is much more to say about blogs than a simple chapter or even a bucketload of perfect phrases will allow. Some reports indicate that around seventy thousand people start new blogs every day, and many more drop or otherwise forget them. Still, there's *lots* of competition out there for blogs. If you want to write a blog, determine *why* you want to write it. To get other people to experience you online? To engage them in a discussion that propels a relationship? In most cases, the likelihood of this occurring is small. However, if you feel compelled to keep a blog as a networking opportunity, then remember the three *E*s: energetic, entertaining, and exclusive.

Keep it energetic, with fast, hip language. Think Slate.com, not an owner's manual.

Do not:
In this blog installment, you will find . . .

Today's blog addresses some of the issues that concern members of my particular field . . .

Do:
Big surprises on the industry front:

So, what's got these professionals hot and bothered—and I don't mean in a good way?

Of course, the "hip" style still has to be true to your voice. You may need to perk up a bit or hone your skills. If you find that your voice is still academic, policy-like, or otherwise dry, then perhaps another form of networking is a better fit for you.

Make sure it's entertaining. No one cares what you had for lunch, but great insights and cool facts told in a fun way will definitely help. Within your blog, you can scatter some of the following:

Myths and realities:
The myth remains that the recent economic failures are the federal government's doing. Yet, the reality is far more frightening than that.

There are many myths about garlic. Ironically, the realities will make you crave it more.

True-and-false statements:
True or false: Friday the 13th is an ancient pagan holiday celebrating sex.

True or false: The first time the Nationals won the championship was in 1964.

Descriptions:
I went to Columbus, Ohio, and saw this grisly sight:

If you go to any manufacturing plant, you see some interesting goings-on that prove efficiency is still not a priority to most plant managers. Here's what I saw on a recent trip to Flatland, Kansas.

It must be exclusive—meaning exclusive to you. It should have your particular style, with a name, visuals, and brand that people will identify as yours.

Here are a few real-life blog names that people use. Notice how different they are and how much they say about their owners:

- Defective Yeti
- Dollarshort
- Dooce
- A Writer's Life
- The Vintage Reader

A successful blog is much like a successful publishing enterprise. You will need to market it and add to it regularly. In fact, with a blog you may be in a particularly strange position of having to network about your networking. So, make sure you enjoy the effort, have time for it, and have plenty to say.

Chapter 12

Websites

In the previous chapter I mentioned that I could write reams about blogs. Ditto for websites. Actually, more than ditto. We could discuss websites for an entire book. Make that a volume of books. Because websites are an amazing networking tool. Get your site up there and the search engines will find you. Then you'll be attracting more people than you've ever dreamed of.

Of course, even without search engines, your site will be a go-to place for people interested in you for practically any reason. You network and what's the first thing they do? Go online and check out your website. Now, a funny thing about websites: the visitor, in this case your contact, decides what he or she thinks about your site relatively quickly—some say in less than the blink of an eye.

So, while the perfect phrases you'll find ahead will definitely help, you should also read how-to books and articles about perfect positioning and perfect visuals for your site. Have a site already? Go back and tweak or, perhaps, even reinvent.

Website Basics and Beyond

Perfect the headlines and subheads that lie beneath them—these are the words that your visitor will see—and respond to—first. They're also what search engines pick up—so add the words your contact would most likely use when trying to find someone like you.

Here are a few tips for intriguing them:

Do not (yawn . . .):
Background Information

What You Should Know

Interesting Facts

And one more "don't": no headers at all. You need headers! They help separate content and increase the likelihood your reader will spend time on the site.

Do:
Check this out!

Today's Feature! [You must update this.]

Hot off the e-press!

Keep the language lively. As we've been discussing throughout this chapter, online networking requires a high level of marketing strategy. The average visitor sees somewhere around seven thousand messages a day: your online presence must compete. So, keep it tight, sharp, and interesting. Ring out every extra word and every extra syllable:

Do not (yawn . . .):
It has been brought to our attention . . .

In the event that you want to seek out more information or otherwise connect with authorities on . . .

Should you want to contact me about these facts, you can reach me at this e-mail address . . .

Do:

Guess what we learned.

Cool links:

E-mail me:

Contact information:

Where to go for even more:

Give them something they want. Make sure the content of your site contains something the visitor is looking for, and quite possibly, something for them to do. That means including podcasts, videos, and links that visitors will use as a resource for themselves, too.

Here are some perfect phrases that point the way:

Listen to my interview with expert Tom Brady.

Don't miss these links:

Great digs:

Sign up for online newsletter:

Special deals with these coupons!

Sign up for regular updates!

You can take this as far as you want. Have contests. Take surveys. Or simply have a link to your online newsletter or updates. Either way, the ultimate networking goal is to "capture" their e-mail addresses. Then, keep in touch!

Use these perfect phrases so visitors will notice (and want) them:

Cool giveaways—just click here!

Fantastic Facts: Fresh to Your E-Box—Sign Up Here!

Your Voice Counts! Take This Survey!

Sign Up for Our Newsletter (It's Amazing!)

Keep in Touch: Sign Up for Our Newsletter

A few concepts are critical here, though:

- If you say you'll send something—coupons, prizes, or even an online newsletter—do it. Never make a promise you can't keep.
- Don't give other people your contacts' information unless the contacts agree that it's OK.
- If you offer a sale or other discount, you must honestly be giving the visitor a break.

The FCC has stringent guidelines about spam, and you must get your contacts' permission to send e-newsletters and an option so they can get off your list. Check out the FCC's website for more.

Getting Leads Through Your Website

The best way to generate leads through your website is to have a site that's so compelling people just naturally talk about it and gravitate toward it. Still, you can encourage them through other means such as links, which we discussed earlier, suggestions on your site, and encouragements such as giving visitors a perk if they send people your way.

Here are some leading lines:

If you get three people to sign up for our newsletter, we'll give you 25% off our next servicing visit.

We want to hear from you—and your friends. Let us know what you like about our website, blog, and newsletter, and we'll send a surprise your way!

How far you go with a marketing slant—and how close you stay to simply discussing yourself and your business—in this case, just ask by using phrases like these:

Tell your friends about us!

Spread the word: Let your friends know about our site and the opportunities to sign up for our newsletter and special deals.

We want to hear from you—and your friends! Click here to add them to our mailing list. (We'll contact them for their approval before adding them!)

Also, be sure to send people *to* your website through your other material. The idea is that they'll see your offers and opportunities once they're there, and the networking wires will click in.

In other materials, be sure to mention specific perks to getting on your site:

To learn more about this important matter, go to . . .

Sign up and get discounts right away.

Get online to learn more!

Want our newsletter? Then go online and sign up!

Check out our list of "Best Buys!" in the Northeast on . . .

Once they're on your site, find straightforward ways to get their information and stay in touch:

Who are you? We want to know. Sign in here!

We want to stay in touch. Tell us who you are.

Want to hear from us? Tell us how we can reach you.

Don't go away—let us know how we can find you.

If you have reluctant visitors, then reassure them in a friendly, upbeat way. You can use words such as:

Trial

Test

Experience

And remind them that they can:

Stop anytime.

Let us know and we'll take you off the list.

Just say no!

Remove your name.

Pull the plug.

You can also have a membership or some sort of social network where visitors need to present their contact information before entering your site. If you're not in the social-networking business, I recommend that you avoid this. It's a lot of work and unless you expend the energy to do it right, you may end up with only three members.

Be sure that you tell them their contact information will be on your list:

We'll add your name to our list.

We'll send you updates and coupons with our e-newsletter every month.

By signing up, you'll be on our list, which entitles you to . . .

Once you complete this information, we'll add your contact information to our e-list and you can begin receiving . . .

Creating Buzz (the Ultimate Networking Opportunity) from Your Website

The concept of buzz is one of the most publicized networking strategies around. In fact, there's more buzz about buzz than actual buzz campaigns. The idea works something like this: if you have an outrageous, mind-numbing, or otherwise intriguing campaign, people will talk (buzz) about it to other people who will check you out and buzz to other people who check you out.

In other words, you're triggering a vast networking response from a simple strategy. Did I say simple? OK, buzz isn't exactly simple, and most organizations and individuals devote a lot of time to launching their buzz initiatives. Still, here are a few ideas that can help—the perfect phrases will naturally emanate from them:

- Give away something cool and intriguing.
- Have a contest that works like a treasure hunt—get newspapers and other online venues to discuss them.
- Offer some type of reward.
- Have cool graphics or outlandish logos.

If the concept of buzz intrigues you, check out the many books and articles about it. You'll find lots of ideas and plenty of case studies that reveal this new marketing-focused means of networking.

Becoming an Authority Through Your Website So People Will Network with You

Make sure your site reveals your level of expertise. While you should have an "About" section that includes your bio, have a short summation somewhere on the home page that people don't have to click on a link to get to. This will encourage others to send links to your site, quote you, even interview you for their blogs and articles and, of course, send people your way.

Start with a few words about what you do:

A prolific author

A foremost authority on . . .

Professor and neurosurgeon

Head chef at . . .

Child care consultant

Nanny with almost twenty years of experience

Consultant and speaker

Adolescent behavior expert

Then state your name and additional details:

. . . has been featured in Educator Today *and other publications.*

. . . trained at the American Culinary Institute.

. . . has been a middle school guidance counselor since 1999.

. . . has appeared on numerous local television and radio shows.

And end with an interesting detail, date, or fact:

He has won the Teacher of the Year Award for three years in a row.

She has worked in fine establishments throughout the country.

He has been certified through Nannies International and is Red Cross trained in emergency rescue.

You can also have regular columns (posts) on your site. Make them timely and fast-paced so people will continue going to your site for more and send other people as well.

Here are some names you can call this column on your site:

Today's Beat!

This Week's Update

Quick Takes

What's New

The Inquisitive Answers

What's to Know

Key In

Link In

Look!

This Week's Buzz

Make sure your columns have regular, timely updates so people will have reason to return (and send others your way). The more frequent the changes and the more visitors you attract, the higher your search engine rating—an amazing networking opportunity.

Start your columns this way:

This week . . .

A big change has occurred . . .

Today . . .

Rumor has it that . . .

New findings have confirmed that . . .

Research reveals that . . .

Then add information that will intrigue your visitor. The column doesn't have to be longer than one or two paragraphs.

Part 4

The Networking-Marketing Marriage

Most people think of traditional marketing as, well, marketing, not networking. Not getting the word out. Not true. In fact, marketing is all about networking: getting people to notice you, contact you, tell other people about you, and add you to their vocabulary. Marketing is the original form of networking, and you can use it in all your networking efforts.

Since so much networking occurs online, you should have all your hard copy marketing materials on your website also. This will help search engines find you and encourage others to spread the word.

Of course, with online networking you can't control how many contacts you'll make or how they find out about you. Through a search? Through someone else's site via a link? It's hard to tell. So, ask! The more you learn about how others find you, the more you can focus on those places and increase your networking efforts.

How you reach people should also depend on *why* you're networking. If you're looking for sales leads or business opportunities, straight marketing works quite well. If you're looking for employment, you won't want a brochure, but you do need a really cool business card. At the very least it will cause contacts to remember you—and recommend you should job possibilities come along.

Chapter 13

Marketing Essentials

Regardless of your vehicle—whether a traditional brochure, a flyer, a bio, or a résumé—every outreach message has similar requirements. You must make them strategic so that contacts are willing to pay attention, make their way through them, and spread the word or otherwise respond appropriately. While this concept may seem more appropriate for, say, longer messages such as cover letters, it's not. Even one-paragraph pieces must be compelling.

Making That First (and Possibly Only) Impression

First impressions are not lasting impressions. Sometimes they're the *only* impression. If the contact isn't hooked from the get-go, then she'll never stick around to read more. I know, I've said that throughout this book—over and over—but it's worth repeating. So, how do you make that lasting impression with your networking material? We discussed this already with the subject lines of e-mails. If you missed that part, go back and take a look. On print messages, here are some other ideas. Most important, you must create a "hook" that's snappy and memorable and immediately apparent.

For Brochures

The hook should go *on the cover*! Most people wait until the inside and lose half their potential audience.

Do not use generic and boring phrases like:

Legal Services

Employment Opportunities

Services

Do use perfect phrases like these:

Solving Legal Problems for 45 Years!

Great Jobs—Amazing Opportunities!

Day and Night Response Team—at Your Service!

You can use your brochure as a networking opportunity by including an invitation of some sort in a place where people can see it, much as you did with online networking:

Half off when you send a friend!

Send a friend our way and come for free.

Special thank-you gifts when you send a friend.

Know someone who'd like to hear from us? Let us know.

Special Invitation: Sign Up a Friend and Come for Free

For Business Cards

Add a short, memorable tagline—something your contact will remember. You can add it to your brochure, website, window displays, and just about everything else.

Here are some examples from websites that are out there today:

The Consumerist: Shoppers bite back.

The Superficial: Because you're ugly.

Scaryduck: Not scary. Not a duck.

The Art of Rhysisms: Chronologically inept since 2060.

The Breakfast Blog: In search of the best eggs in town.

You can also learn from the classics, although your tagline doesn't have to be quite so musical or spiffy:

Purdue's tagline: "It takes a tough man to make a tender chicken."

Peter Paul Mounds Bars: "Sometime you feel like a nut, sometimes you don't."

The classic Star Trek line: "To boldly go where no man has gone before."

Timex's tagline since 1956: "It takes a licking and keeps on ticking."

Winston cigarettes: "Winston tastes good like a cigarette should."

You don't have to be overly spiffy or cool—you are networking, after all, and not creating a million-dollar ad campaign. Still, you want contacts to remember you. When you hand them a business card, you want them to pass it on!

Keep it simple, if that works:

Toxic spills expert

No. 1 UVV Sales Representative

25 Years in Water Testing

Joyce Award Winner 2009

For Résumés or Other Biographical Material

State your most impressive attribute where the contact can see it. Do *not* wedge it into the piece or hide it by starting with, say, a date or number unless that number is important.

Just say no:
For several years, clients have benefited from . . .

I have been engaged in various . . .

My track record is worth noting . . .

Do this instead:
For 25 years, clients have benefited from . . .

From 50,000 cases to a few dollars' investment, we have helped a variety of clients . . .

As an award-winning . . .

For Handouts Such as Flyers and Covers on Training Materials

Don't miss this opportunity. On the cover, say something intriguing about yourself so the contacts will remember you—and spread the word to colleagues, bosses, and friends. Besides, they may pass along your material, as well as a good word, so you want the cover to intrigue, entice, and stick.

State your name and any degrees or other helpful information:

Arthur Jones, Ph.D.

Samantha Ferrisky, author, **The Finer Touch**

Don Hanley, sales consultant

If your employer's name is helpful (assuming you're not network-ing to get a job), mention that:

William O'Reilly, Senior Vice President, AccuCenter

Miriam Hotspot, President, Diligent Association

Martha Hadley, Office Manager, Hillard&Hillard

Then choose an interesting and eye-catching title so contacts know exactly what you do and how you can benefit them:

Do not:
Finding Employees

Better Writing

Safe Travel

Do:
Leading Strategies for Finding Better Employees, Faster

Effective Communications for Faster, More Cost-Effective Results

Global Travel Risk Management Specialist

And, of course, include all your contact information right on the page, including your e-mail address and website. If you're job hunting, include your Facebook, MySpace, or other Web presence.

Building Credibility

One of the greatest problems with talking about yourself is this: who's going to believe you? Naturally, no one's about to say: "I'm a total jerk, but am hoping to get leads anyway." So, how do you and your networking efforts have the credibility to get the response you want? The answer: Let other people speak for you.

If you have a blog or website, people may comment. If you're lucky, these comments will be good and raise your credibility. If not—well, let's not discuss. (Don't even *think* of putting in your own comments—it's tacky.) But hard copy material is much more stagnant and you can't rely on the "kindness of strangers" as you might online. So, here's what you do:

Include Testimonials

Pick through these carefully, so you have really reliable and specific testimonials. These should include before and after examples, if possible. How you get this type of information is up to you; the best bet is to have the source send you the testimonial, then you tweak it. Don't use anything without that person's OK. You can also write the testimonial for people and get their approval and changes, if that's easier for them.

Your testimonials should be about four or five lines long and look something like this:

She brought results three or four times faster than anyone in the past.

We were amazed: our profits went up twice as high within two months of Charlie's arrival.

At first, we didn't think we'd find a solution. Then . . .

We really looked forward to the results. But these were better than we anticipated. What happened was . . .

Add Case Studies

Case studies should be a few paragraphs long and indicate the problem your client or employer was trying to solve, the methodology you used to solve the problem, and the results you achieved. *But*—who's going to read an entire case study? So start each one with a quick overview that's so easy to read your audience won't even have to move their eyes.

Here are some examples—use the structure as well as the introductory words and phrases:

Problem: *Corrupt data throughout system causing costly delays*

Methodology: *Applied the HYG Data Management System*

Results: *Solved 75% of the problems within six months, cutting related expenses by 45%*

Problem: *Major losses of advertising revenue threatened magazine's existence*

Methodology: *Reconfigured advertising model*

Results: *Advertising dollars up 100% at height of recession*

Problem: *Air quality was poor in the general RA region*

Methodology: *Analysis and review of environmental factors*

Results: *Air quality has consistently improved over the past 24 months.*

Note how these statements are specific and clear. If you don't have an immediate result, dig a little. You're bound to find some. Otherwise, don't bother with the case study.

Supply Quotes

As with testimonials, you can get someone to draft you a quote, take it from a letter of recommendation, pull it from reviews that you have had in the past, or develop one that you show the person for her OK. You can focus on your personality as well as your professional successes or skill set. If you're at a networking meeting, do include these in your packet!

> *He's an easygoing person even under intense pressure.*
>
> *What a find! I wish I could take her everywhere!*
>
> *Her conscientious approach and diligent follow-through brought us amazing results!*
>
> *One of the best employees we ever had! The worst part about moving headquarters was that she couldn't come with us!*

Include Awards and Other Tributes

As long as it's good, awards and other tributes can't hurt. If the contacts won't know an acronym, spell it out.

> *2009 Winner of the Best in Class*
>
> *Received the President's Award for Exceptional Service*
>
> *Honored by the National Association of Associations*
>
> *Won top honors at Brandeis University Executive Service Event*

Engaging the Contact

You can engage the contact by using a few simple strategies. These will help him have a stronger experience when reading your message and have a more enduring memory of you. Remember, really good networking doesn't last for an hour, but for years and years. You want the contact to pass your name around every time a need comes up and to send leads and referrals, as well.

Speak to the reader directly:

Ever notice that every time you solve the problem, it crops up again?

You probably have wondered the same thing yourself.

You may have heard of us—most people have. Here's why:

You can find more about me, plus plenty of helpful tips, on my website, blog, or Facebook account.

Use metaphors: they tap into contacts' senses and help them remember you:

We can shovel away those remaining problems, and you'll never see them again.

We've learned that flying is better than crawling.

You can practically see the coal turn to diamonds.

Your livelihood is more than a math problem.

Leave some issues open-ended—then resolve them:

But, did you know how that translates into dollars?

Are you ready to take this trip?

But the question remains: how do we achieve this? The answer:

The amount of overdue penalties will astound you. It's . . .

Creating a Message That Encourages a Response

While marketing, and all other types of networking material, is good, it's ultimately useless unless you get the response you want. So, think through your mission and be clear about the outcome. Do you want the person to send you numerous contacts? Pass your information along to a particular contact, such as a senior VP or other decision makers? Or do you simply want to make an enduring impression, so that should the opportunity arrive, they'll think of you?

Once you've determined the result you want, determine a strategy that will help.

The response: Send your contacts to your website

The purpose: To give you their—and other people's—contact information to expand your network

How to achieve this: Make an offer they can't refuse and can only get online

The phrases:

Go online and get a 10% discount.

Online you'll find some helpful tips from the foremost authorities in the business.

On our website you'll see links and other helpful information that could change your life.

Go online for much more.

Once there, they'll immediately have the opportunity to give you their contact information—and that of others. Then, add the addresses to your mailing list and save any personal information so you know more about who's responding, why, and who you should target. It will also tell you if you're *not* reaching your best networking target.

The response: Give information to their senior-level managers
The purpose: So they will contact you or, more likely, will take
    your call later
How to achieve this: Show how you'll make their work life better
    should the senior guy invite you in

Here are some perfect phrases:

*I've seen that problem many times. Take a look at my
material and why not give a packet to your boss. You'll see
case studies that show some of our successes.*

*Maybe I should talk to your boss about some solutions? Why
don't I give you these materials as a greeting and you can
pass them along.*

*I'd really like to talk to your manager. You shouldn't have to
devote so much wasteful time to doing this.*

*That must be frustrating. There are lots of alternatives. If you
like, I can meet with you and your boss to discuss them. In the
meantime, here's some information that may help.*

You could always hand the person your business card and call him
later. But handing some material—especially a packet that contains
helpful information for him or his company (not just advertising material about you)—will leave a more enduring impression. And—give
him your business card.

Getting a Direct Response

In many cases, you want the contact to do something immediately—
right then and there. For example, you may want her to give you
contact information, take a survey, or give you lead names. This can
be tricky as you don't want to embarrass yourself if she says no or put

her in an uncomfortable position where she must say yes. Marketing material can help here. The professional look and interesting positioning will encourage contacts to engage with you and see that you're legitimate. Here are some ideas of what you can do.

Talk to them and make them feel you are comfortable asking for something right away. Then, show them how they will help you by giving you insights:

I'd really appreciate your giving us insights into . . .

Could you provide some information? It would be really helpful to us.

Would you mind . . .

I'd really appreciate your . . .

Then, show them the advantage to you. Feeling like they've helped can be enough, but see if you can sweeten the deal, too:

We'll give you . . .

As a thank-you we'll send you a . . .

We'd like to provide you with . . .

As thanks, I'd like you to have . . .

To say thank you, I'd like to give you . . .

Would you like . . .

Next, ask for their contact information.

Can we keep in touch?

I'd like to have your contact information, if that's OK.

Would you like me to follow up?

We have sales and interesting opportunities all the time. How can we get in touch with you?

Would you like us to update you about opportunities like these?

Promise not to add them to any list without their approval first:

We won't add you to our list unless we have your approval first.

I'd like to send you our newsletter but will get your online approval first.

We'll send you updates. If you don't want them, just let us know.

We'll put you on our list but will get your approval before we start sending you anything.

Then, ask if they know anyone else who should be on your list. If appropriate, supply incentives:

Do you know anyone else who would enjoy . . . ?

Can you think of anyone else who might like . . . ?

We'd like to contact some of your friends, too. If you give us two names, we'll give all of you a . . .

Do you have any friends who . . . ?

Can you think of any colleagues who might like to hear from us? We'll get their approval before sending them anything.

As always, when you make a promise to get their approval first, keep it.

Chapter 14

Brochures, Invitations, Sales Calls, and Letters

Using Brochures to Get People to Call or E-Mail

We already discussed brochures in the previous chapter, but they're worth a deeper look. While brochures are old school, they still have a lot of networking jazz. They can be the perfect vehicle for sending people—and their friends—your way. The primary consideration in creating successful brochures is the "usability" quota. Keep reading to find out what I mean.

Creating Brochures with a High "Usability" Factor

The term "usability" refers to creating content that people can really use. You can provide tips, lists of resources, and calendars of specific dates.

Make sure that your contacts are aware of how much your brochure will benefit them by having strong and informative headers:

The Ten Most Important Numbers to Leave on Your Fridge

Five Ways to Keep Your Heating Bills Low

Tip for Finding (and Keeping) a Good Nanny

Then, tell them how they can learn or get more, and get them to go on your site:

To find more tips and other valuable information, go to our website and click on . . .

Want more? We have dozens of other tips at . . .

For more invaluable contact numbers, go to . . .

On your site, you can also have a spot for contact information that says something like:

Know someone who would appreciate these tips? Give us his address and we'll send them along.

We're always eager to spread the word. Give us the addresses and we'll send this helpful advice to your friends.

Get them to call you:

Call us at (800) 888-8000 between 9:00 A.M. and 5:00 P.M. and we'll send you tip sheets and other materials.

Still have questions? Just call and we'll provide answers.

Need more? Give us a call—we'll be happy to talk to you and get you what you need.

Although not viral, phone calls are exceptionally interpersonal, especially for the baby boomer crowd. So plan on engaging your contact in conversation. You can get information, learn more about what works or doesn't work in your networking approach, and even garner leads or ideas to help propel you forward.

Get them to e-mail you:

Just e-mail us for more.

Like our brochure? You'll love our tip sheets. Just e-mail us and we'll e-mail them back!

We're here and ready to send you more at . . .

Like what you see? Let us know and we'll give you more. Just e-mail us at . . .

Once they e-mail you, you'll have their contact information. Save it and, with their approval, start the networking gears in motion through reminders, newsletters, updates, and requests for contacts.

Get them to snail-mail you—this is especially helpful with brief questionnaires. You can also use your website for communication:

Just fill in the questionnaire and drop it in the mail or send it to us through our website . . .

Tell us a little about yourself by answering these questions. Send us your contact information, and we'll send you . . .

Creating Networking Opportunities Through Sales Letters

The trick to using sales letters as a networking tool is to ensure that your letter is timely:

This weekend only . . .

Call us now—don't miss this opportunity!

July 4 weekend only!

It must have a specific destination or outcome:

Attend our onetime sale . . .

Join us for a sales event unlike any other.

Come see our new line of . . .

You can compel your readers to come and bring friends:

Bring a friend and get an additional 10% off.

Guests get an additional 5% off.

Bringing guests? They'll be treated to . . .

Or simply make a suggestion:

Let us know if you want to bring friends.

You are welcome to bring friends.

Try this for a feeling of exclusivity:

Guests are welcome—but no more than two per person.

Please limit your friends to two each.

When possible, create a clublike feeling so your contact will want to participate in your sale or event:

. . . and bring this letter to get in!

Join our Special Customer Club.

Discriminating customers like you!

Our best customers!

For people with good taste—like you!

So, what's the difference between sales and networking? With sales, you try to sell something. With networking, you try to reach as many people as possible—and have them reach as many people as possible—to expand your reputation, your breadth, and, of course, your profits or whatever else you're after.

Creating Networking Opportunities Through Cold Calls

Cold calls have a really bad rap—which is unfortunate. They're among the best ways to get information you need about a potential client, customer, or even contact. Being on the phone creates an interactive dynamic that can lead you to get the information you want—information you can get in no better way.

Start by introducing yourself, and add whatever interesting title or affiliation will intrigue them most:

I'm the former president of the Dog and Cat Lovers Association.

I wrote several books on personality tests.

I received my degree from . . .

I own a . . .

I'm the former . . .

I'm a . . .

I won a large . . .

I'm the president of a . . .

If you've been in the news or have a strong online presence, you might mention that; sound like you're trying to draw a connection, not brag:

You may have seen my article in . . .

You may have read about me in . . .

If you get the Boston Globe, then you may have seen the article about me last week.

I have a pretty popular blog.

I am frequently quoted in . . .

I used to host . . .

I taught at . . .

Whatever it is, your mission is to build credibility, create openness, possibly spur a conversation. But to win any of this, you must be brief. As in a few words—not a minibiography.

Let them know you're not making a sales call—directly or indirectly:

This isn't a sales call.

This is an informational call only.

Ask for the information you need—politely:

I was wondering if you could tell me . . .

Would you happen to know . . .

I wanted to . . ., but I wasn't sure about the best steps to take.

Can you explain how . . .

Do you know . . .

Can you give me any insights about . . .

Since I'm new to the area, I wasn't sure about . . .

I've tried before but may have taken the wrong step . . .

Thank them or otherwise show appreciation after they give you choice tidbits of information or at the end of the call:

That's really interesting, thanks.

I never thought of that.

Wow—that's amazing. Who knew?

Thank you—that was quite helpful.

Great.

Interesting.

I never would have thought of that.

Why haven't any of the books I've read included that?

Follow up when appropriate—by phone or e-mail:

I contacted you last week. Thought you'd like to know that since then . . .

Don't know if you remember me, but we talked last fall. Since then, I've . . .

Just wanted to update you since that helpful phone call last month.

As always, give credit where it's due:

You were incredibly helpful.

Thanks to your good advice, I was able to . . .

You sent me to Mr. Faber, who referred me to Jake Smith. That contact fueled more opportunities than you can imagine.

Your advice was amazing.

After I received your advice, I . . .

Thanks to your advice, I . . .

With your contacts, I was able to delve deeper and get great results.

Reaching the Decision Maker Through a Cold Call

Cold calls can be an amazing way to reach decision makers—although you may need an indirect approach. Your best friend can be the least expected: the gatekeeper. If he gives the nod (and advice such as when to call), you're in. If not, he may be able to send you to someone else who will help.

Ask for help, and use the person's full name. This makes the call seem genuine.

Do not:
I need to talk to the senior VP.

Is the CEO in?

Could you tell me when I could reach a decision maker?

Do you know when a person in charge will be around?

Is the VP of Human Resources in, by any chance?

Also do not:

Could you tell me his or her name, please?

Who would that person be?

What is his or her name?

I'm not sure who that is. Can you tell me a little about him?

Who?

What was that name?

How do you pronounce that?

Hmm—interesting name.

Do:

I was wondering if you could help me. I need to talk to Dr. Silverman. Do you know how I could find him?

Is Adam Joseph in, by any chance? I know he's busy, but I was hoping to talk to him.

I need to talk to Ms. Robb. Can you give me any advice about the best way to reach her?

Do you think you could connect me to Maria Frank?

I needed to talk to Henry Holt. Do you know how I could reach him?

Is Mr. Farley in? When do you think he'll be in?

Explain why, but keep it short:

I just need information about the company's . . .

I read an article about him and wanted to follow up.

I wanted to inform her that . . .

Whenever possible, present the discussion as benefiting the decision maker:

I have a unique approach I think might interest her.

I was hoping to join the company because I have a particular set of experiences . . .

I can provide some helpful insights. Fleebonker and Whittle were my clients and I know the industry well.

Set a time limit:

I'd only take ten minutes.

I just needed a few ideas.

I was hoping to get five minutes.

I just wanted to know . . .

Ask when you should call back or e-mail:

What is the best way to reach her?

When should I call?

Which works best—a call, text message, or e-mail?

Should I contact her early in the morning?

I can drop by briefly, if that works best.

If you are told the person is impossible to reach, get another name—or two or three:

Do you know someone else I can call?

Is there someone else I could talk to?

Do you know anyone else who could give me insights?

Who else do you think I should talk to?

Is there a better person for me to reach?

Do you know anyone there who might be available briefly?

As always, say thanks!

I appreciate your help.

Thanks for your insights.

Thank you.

Chapter 15

Buried Networking Opportunities

Send Invitations No One (and Their Friends) Can Resist

Invitations are an amazing way to get people to attend an event, bring friends, and spread the word. While at your event, they'll leave their contact information, add friends to your list, experience your product or service, and spread the word even more! You don't want to have more than two or three events a year (otherwise the novelty will wear off), and they should always, always, always be experiences to remember.

Invite them by U.S. mail or e-mail, using a formal or informal voice depending on your style and theirs:

You are cordially invited to an open house . . .

Guess what? We're having a party and you're invited!

It's that time of year again! Our spring "jump for joy" event!

It's time again for our ice-cream fest—hurry before it melts!

Make them feel as if the event is special, using words like:

Exclusive

By invitation only

Annual

Special guest

Be our guest

Honored to invite you

Onetime

Make sure the event is timely, which should fuel their interest and let them know the opportunity is limited:

Our annual invitation-only spring event

Our fall collection party

Our ground hog celebration!

The annual come-as-you-are event

If your invite list isn't too long, call to follow up. If it is, then call select invitees—the ones with the most networking clout. Here's what you'll say:

Just calling to see if you can make our May 4 event.

Are you planning to come to the Post–New Year's Party?

We're having a small gathering to show this year's fashion line. Will you be attending?

We're counting heads for the preview party. Will we see you there?

Do you think you can make the May Day celebration? It should be fun.

Don't forget to invite them to bring a guest:

Will you be bringing a guest?

How many of you will there be?

How many guests will you bring? [A leading question, but it may encourage them!]

Want to bring a few friends?

Were you going to bring friends?

We're happy to have you bring friends—how many do you expect to bring?

Would you like us to send invitations to any of your friends?

Add the friends to your network by having a sign-in sheet. Be polite and hospitable:

Would you mind signing in?

Are you a friend of Jane's? Great. Have you signed in yet?

Would you mind signing in? We'd like to know more about you.

Care to sign our guest list?

Let them know they'll be on your mailing list; present this as a privilege (which it will be!) and not a pain:

By signing up, you'll get to receive notices about upcoming sales and other events.

Once you sign up, you'll receive special coupons. Sign up a friend, and they'll receive coupons, too!

We'll send you our monthly newsletter with tips, links, and cool facts you won't want to miss.

You can also use words like:

Entitles you to . . .

Gives you the opportunity to . . .

Gives you exclusive . . .

Puts you on our select customer list . . .

Use Text Messaging

It's true that text messaging is the best way to reach kids—as opposed to, say, baby boomers. Still, the networking potential of these virtual gems are only beginning to be touched. Here are a few ideas and perfect phrases to make them work.

Have contacts agree to receive text messages alerting them to a free pass or gift opportunity:

Want us to text you about our sales and special offers?

We'll send you a text message for up-to-the-minute deals.

Learning about great opportunities is a text message away!

Text them about special deals such as getting in free to a concert, club, or interesting talk if they bring a friend. If you own a restaurant, then the people you're texting can get a meal for half price if they bring friends.

Here are some texts:

Guess what! Half off tonight!

Good deal—today only!

Text us back and you'll get . . .

Text us and let us know if you can attend!

Bring a friend and you'll get in free.

Send us a friend and you'll get in free.

Sign on a friend for our Text Alerts and you both get . . .

Be sure to extend the offer to other friends.

Use Surveys to Open Doors

While these babies aren't a direct networking opportunity, they can help you network in the future. By knowing who the good contacts for you are and why they network about you in the first place, you'll be able to focus your efforts.

Request a response:

We want to give you the service you desire—so please, fill out this survey and tell us what you want.

How are we doing? Please let us know!

We want to know. Please fill out this short survey.

What do you think? Ten questions—tell us all!

We'd love to hear from you.

When possible, offer them something in return.

Ask the right questions—be sure to veer to the positive:

Do not:

What don't you like about our service?

What will make our product better?

What problems have you experienced that we should know about?

What do you think about our prices? Are they too high?

Do:

Why do you choose our product?

What do you like about our service?

What more would you like us to provide?

What is the best aspect of our pricing?

What other aspects of our service would you like us to know about?

Plus, ask them:

How did you hear about us?

How long have you been a customer?

What do you like most about our special offers?

Where do you purchase our product? Online? In stores?

It's always helpful to get demographic information:

What is your birth date?

What is your address?

Do you prefer to be contacted by phone? E-mail? Text message?

Do you have children? If so, what are their ages?

Do you work? At home? For someone else?

Follow up later with the results:

We thought you'd be interested in the results of our survey.

We calculated the results of the survey you took; we wanted to pass on the highlights.

Thank you for helping with our survey. The findings are amazing—and we're sending you the highlights.

We appreciate your help with our survey. Thanks to your input, we have made the following changes!

Also include ways you can further develop the relationship:

We have added you to our mailing list. If you would also like to receive our two-for-the-price-of-one mailers, please let us know.

Do you have friends who would like to receive our two-for-the-price-of-one mailers?

As a thank-you, we'd like to invite you and a friend to our exclusive wine tasting.

We'd like to offer you and a friend the chance to . . .

Remind them of special deals involving others:

We'll give you a free sample of Priceless—our star product according to our survey—every time a friend or family member tells us you sent them.

We'll give you and a friend half off of . . .

We'll provide you a 25% discount of our feature product every time you bring them into our store. Send two friends—even better—we'll give you 50% off!

Our survey proved that customers think our prices are low and our quality is high. As a thank-you for this and other information, we invite you and two friends to . . .

Host Contests and Challenges—They Work!

One of the best networking options is the most fun—contests and challenges. They range from the fish bowl lotteries you see at trade shows, where people put their names and contact information on a slip of paper and you pull a winner, to intricate treasure hunts where they must go online or find clues on the wrappers of your products.

While deciding on a contest or challenge, be sure to consider important factors that could make or break your success.

Here are some critical factors to consider:

How much time can you devote to the contest or challenge?

How good will the prize be? The better the prize the more likely people will participate.

How many resources do you have who will help? The more employees, the better.

Do you have "partners" who will help, such as shops or online communities where you can announce your contest or challenge for no cost?

Do you have PR experience? A press release to a newspaper or online publication will certainly help spread the word.

Announce the contest, prize first:

Win an amazing trip to . . .

A beautiful, handmade quilt will be yours if . . .

You can win this prize by . . .

Sign up to win a . . .

This bicycle is all yours if you win our Summer Challenge!

Next, tell them what they have to do to win. Do not make it sound like an exam or requirements on an insurance policy by avoiding these words:

Must . . .

Are required to . . .

Are responsible for . . .

Are obligated to . . .

Will be immediately disqualified if . . .

Must adhere to the rules . . .

As in:

You must sign up by 11/14 or you cannot enter the contest.

It is imperative that you complete all the information on the contest form or you will be disqualified.

Complete the form in its entirety.

This contest involves sending in an essay for our judges to review. Be sure to have perfect punctuation and spelling or your essay will be disqualified.

Do keep it upbeat and compelling:

Just follow the rules . . .

Complete the form and you're in!

Send in your essay—keep the spelling and punctuation accurate. Otherwise we might miss your good thoughts!

We want to know all about you, so be sure to complete all sections of the short form.

Make it sound risky, cool, and, yes, fun—especially if it involves a challenge. These words will help:

Challenge

Dare

Invite

Spot

Find

Determine

Figure out

Can you

Do you dare to

Bet you can't

See if you can

Want to try

Go ahead and try

As in:

We challenge you to . . .

Think you can figure out where the marbles are hidden?

See if you can spot the problems.

Here's a puzzle we challenge you to get!

Go ahead and try to guess the answer! If you get it, you'll win these amazing prizes.

Give them a reason to give you contact information:

We want to learn more about you.

We'll e-mail you the names of the winners and the correct answers.

Want to try our other contests? Then give us your contact information and we'll let you know when and where!

If the contest is fun and the prize worthwhile, the buzz will naturally start humming and people will do the networking for you. Before you know it, you'll have hundreds of new names from a single contest. Even those fish bowl lotteries at trade shows that I mentioned earlier will bring in lots of new names if the prize is tempting.

Create a Club with Special Advantages

Creating a club can be the best way around to get more-than-willing leads. Communications companies, for example, have set up great networking strategies through their clubs—which they call "plans." They have "family plans" and "friends and family plans" and plenty of others. What's most amazing about this opportunity is that the phone companies have tapped the full potential of networking—getting people to network for them *and* sign up for their plan!—without having to do much more than have ads.

No matter what you call them, you can start your club this way. First, figure out a name that explains the arrangement. Here are some ideas; you've seen some of these around, I'm sure:

Sam's Club

Preferred Customers

Perfect Drivers Plan

Friends Plan

You and a Friend Club

Then determine a deal. It can't be a one-shot deal; it must be regular, if not daily:

You and your friends will get a year of services for half off by signing up for our Perfect Friends Club.

Sign up—and bring a friend—and you'll receive text messages every month announcing an exclusive sale.

By joining our Perfect Customer Club you'll get special discounts and free gifts. Invite a friend and we'll sweeten the deal.

Sign up for our Sweeter than Candy Club and send your friends and family monthly sweet treats. And you'll get some yourself!

Tell people about it everywhere:

Sign up for our year-round Sweetheart Club!

Are you a Perfect Customer? If so, join our Perfect Customer Club.

If you have a store, remind them.

Discounts for club members only

Special Club member discounts today

Sign up and receive bonus points today

As you may know from the supermarket "membership" cards and similar programs, you can offer points that give your contacts discounts, freebies, and deals that will win their loyalty so they keep coming back. You can encourage customers to network on your behalf by offering them extra points for every new member they sign on!

And remember: use your imagination, always. Networking isn't an approach but a way of living in the professional world. Every opportunity offers a new and intriguing possibility to make new contacts and expand your reach.

The Right Phrase for Every Situation...Every Time

Perfect Phrases for Building Strong Teams
Perfect Phrases for Business Letters
Perfect Phrases for Business Proposals and Business Plans
Perfect Phrases for Business School Acceptance
Perfect Phrases for College Application Essays
Perfect Phrases for Cover Letters
Perfect Phrases for Customer Service
Perfect Phrases for Dealing with Difficult People
Perfect Phrases for Dealing with Difficult Situations at Work
Perfect Phrases for Documenting Employee Performance Problems
Perfect Phrases for Executive Presentations
Perfect Phrases for Landlords and Property Managers
Perfect Phrases for Law School Acceptance
Perfect Phrases for Lead Generation
Perfect Phrases for Managers and Supervisors
Perfect Phrases for Managing Your Small Business
Perfect Phrases for Medical School Acceptance
Perfect Phrases for Meetings
Perfect Phrases for Motivating and Rewarding Employees
Perfect Phrases for Negotiating Salary & Job Offers
Perfect Phrases for Perfect Hiring
Perfect Phrases for the Perfect Interview
Perfect Phrases for Performance Reviews
Perfect Phrases for Real Estate Agents & Brokers
Perfect Phrases for Resumes
Perfect Phrases for Sales and Marketing Copy
Perfect Phrases for the Sales Call
Perfect Phrases for Setting Performance Goals
Perfect Phrases for Small Business Owners
Perfect Phrases for the TOEFL Speaking and Writing Sections
Perfect Phrases for Writing Grant Proposals
Perfect Phrases in American Sign Language for Beginners
Perfect Phrases in French for Confident Travel
Perfect Phrases in German for Confident Travel
Perfect Phrases in Italian for Confident Travel
Perfect Phrases in Spanish for Confident Travel to Mexico
Perfect Phrases in Spanish for Construction
Perfect Phrases in Spanish for Gardening and Landscaping
Perfect Phrases in Spanish for Household Maintenance and Child Care
Perfect Phrases in Spanish for Restaurant and Hotel Industries

Visit mhprofessional.com/perfectphrases for a complete product listing.

Learn more. Do more.